The Devil
ON TRIAL

The Devil ON TRIAL

WITCHES, ANARCHISTS, ATHEISTS, COMMUNISTS, AND TERRORISTS IN AMERICA'S COURTROOMS

BY PHILLIP MARGULIES AND MAXINE ROSALER

HOUGHTON MIFFLIN COMPANY ✛ BOSTON 2008

www.houghtonmifflinbooks.com

The text of this book is set in Adobe Caslon Pro 12.5 point.
Photo credits appear on page 209.

Library of Congress Cataloging-in-Publication Data
Margulies, Phillip.
  The devil on trial : witches, anarchists, atheists, communists, and terrorists
in America's courtrooms / by Phillip Margulies and Maxine Rosaler.
    p. cm.
  ISBN 978-0-618-71717-0
  1. Trials—United States. 2. Criminal justice, Administration of—Social aspects—
United States. 3. Discrimination in criminal justice administration—United States—
History. I. Rosaler, Maxine. II. Title.
  KF220.M27 2008
345.73'02—dc22

                      2008001870

Printed in the United States of America
MP 10 9 8 7 6 5 4 3 2

Contents

The U.S. Supreme Court Building, Washington, D.C.

Introduction

Every so often a trial comes along that grips an entire nation, or even the entire world, with the spectacle of absolute evil being held to account for its crimes—evil, that is, as defined at the particular time during which the trial takes place. A spy who has sold secrets to the enemy, an anarchist trying to start a revolution, a terrorist who has caused the deaths of thousands of innocent people—defendants like these become symbols of something greater than the crime of which they are accused. They represent a threat that faces the community as a whole, the one thing that everyone fears. They represent the devil.

Almost everyone has a good idea of what they want to occur at such a trial. They want to see a drama of justice unfold. They want to see the cunning plotter blink helplessly in the light of the courtroom, confronted with the victims he has wronged or with the survivors who mourn the victims. They want to watch the devil squirm in his seat as he listens to the testimony against him, to hear him sputter unconvincingly on the witness stand, to see him tremble before the People's judgment. They want to see the scales balanced and the world made right again.

What most people *don't* want is for the devil to be found not guilty simply because there isn't enough proof that he committed the particular crime of which he stands accused. When the defendant is the devil, only one verdict is acceptable.

In the grip of the great fears that these trials dramatize, prosecutors tend to forget that the legal system itself has to operate within the limits of the law. Eager to win at any cost, they may remind the jurors that the accused is a member of a vast conspiracy that will do anything to accomplish its purposes, a threat so grave that—the prosecutor may hint without exactly saying it—it is all right, just this once, to pronounce the guilty verdict we *know* is true even if the evidence doesn't quite prove it. For this is a unique emergency (so this kind of logic runs). It is a struggle for survival.

Before the trial has even begun, newspapers have reached a verdict and so has the public. It can take months to find twelve people willing to say they will listen to the case with an open mind. And during the trial, when there is a dispute between the lawyers on the admissibility of a piece of evidence, judges may be tempted to deliver the popular ruling instead of the fair one. In a time of fear, it is difficult to be fair.

DEVILS OF THE AMERICAN PAST

Later, when the furor has died down and years have passed, trials in which the defendants were symbols of absolute evil evoke a fascination of a different kind. Thanks to the passions that surrounded them, these trials speak to us of a vanished generation, people now long dead who thought they had the devil in their midst. For each era has its own devil, quite different from the devil of another time.

Back in 1692, in Salem, Massachusetts, the devil was the actual, literal devil and those who had made a pact with him. In the years since then, America's enemy within has taken the form of bomb-throwing anarchists, teachers of evolution, Communists, and terrorists.

FAIR TRIAL FOR THE DEVIL

Looking back at these trials, we do not necessarily think all the defendants were as innocent as we now know the "witches" of Salem were. Some of the threats were very real. And in retrospect, some of the trials were fair and some were not. Yet all the trials in this book had one thing in common: each one was a response to the special problems that confront a democracy when it thinks it is putting the devil on trial. In some cases, that challenge was met successfully; in other cases, it was not, and in that respect each of these trials can be seen as a kind of medical instrument that tested the health of American democracy at the time it took place.

The great challenge, always, is to give the devil a *fair* trial. A trial that is rigged in advance to make certain that the defendant does not escape cannot be fair. In a democracy, when the devil goes on trial, the democracy goes on trial as well.

This is the lesson in the law that has to be relearned in every generation. As a nation of immigrants, the United States is unified not by religion, race, or custom but by its devotion to specific ideals of equality and human rights. Our courtrooms are not merely the places where people and companies sue one another and where criminals are judged. They are the places where our country either succeeds or fails to live up to its ideals. The court is an institution as central to democracy as the vote.

Etched into the marble of the Supreme Court building in Washington, DC, are the words "Equal Justice Under Law." That is the central ideal the United States is supposed to live by, the ideal in its abstract purity. The episodes that follow in these pages show how this precious goal of equal justice—justice even for the devil himself—worked out, for better or for worse, in the murk of real life, among imperfect people gripped by the great terrors of their day, facing the unknown future, fighting for their lives.

"Sarah Good . . . Why do you thus torment these poor children?"—*John Hathorne*

"We ourselves were not capable to understand, nor able to withstand the mysterious delusions of the Power of Darkness, and the Prince of the Air." —*Written statement of the Salem Witch Trial jurors on the Day of Humiliation, January 14, 1697*

A nineteenth-century painting by T. H. Matteson depicting the Salem witch trials.

✤ *Chapter 1* ✤
The Salem Witch Trials

In every generation, there has always been some feared group to play the role of the devil in the American imagination. In 1692, in the little English colony of Massachusetts, the role of the devil was played by . . . the Devil . . . and by those who were said to have signed their name in his book. Once the accusations began to fly, anyone who questioned the justice of the trials was asking to join the ranks of the accused.

THE BEWITCHMENT

The winter of 1692 was the coldest to afflict New England in years. Water froze in pots and buckets, and the surfaces of wells had to be broken up with axes. In the meetinghouse where the God-fearing inhabitants of Salem, Massachusetts, attended religious services, even the sacramental bread froze, making a harsh rattling sound when it was dropped onto the sacramental plates. In fruitless searches for warmth, worshipers draped blankets across their laps, placed pans of hot coals beneath the benches where they sat, and nestled their feet under the bellies of their dogs. Sometimes, the only way for the pious villagers to escape the bitter cold was to leave the meetinghouse altogether and go home to seek whatever meager warmth their fireplaces had to offer.

That January the villagers were confronted by an uncanny series of events which added fear of the unknown and a conviction of spreading evil to the discomforts already experienced by the community. The trouble began when two girls living in the household of the village minister, Samuel Parris, started to behave very strangely. Betty Parris, the minister's daughter, was the first to exhibit the odd symptoms. She began to forget things and would fidget nervously during religious services. When her father scolded her for failing to keep her mind on her prayer, she would bark like a dog. Instead of reciting her evening prayers, she spewed forth gibberish. She threw her Bible against the wall.

Soon her orphaned cousin Abigail, adopted into the Parris household, started having fits, too. Abigail would run around the house flapping her arms and trying to fly, shouting, "Whish! Whish!" Once she tried to fly up the chimney.

Samuel Parris summoned a group of doctors to the house. None of them could find a medical explanation for the girls' strange behavior. Finally, Dr. Samuel Griggs made the diagnosis that would lead to the most famous series of trials in American history. Within a period of less than a year, nineteen innocent men and women—and two dogs—would be hanged for an invisible crime. More than a hundred innocent people, including a four-year-old child, would be imprisoned for months, chained to the walls of dark, rat-infested dungeons, and one man would be forced to lie naked on the ground while heavy stones were piled onto his chest until he died.

Condemned witches being hung in a public square in Europe.

The doctor set this chain of events into motion when he declared, "The evil hand is upon them." In his professional opinion, the girls were bewitched.

No one thought it odd that a learned man would make such a statement, for belief in witchcraft was all but universal in 1692. In fact, the Salem witch trials were the last of a great wave of witch trials conducted throughout the mid-sixteenth and seventeenth centuries, almost all of them in Europe. Witchcraft was a crime punishable by death, and during the previous two centuries, as many as one hundred thousand people in the Old World were executed for being witches.

When literate New Englanders wanted to know more

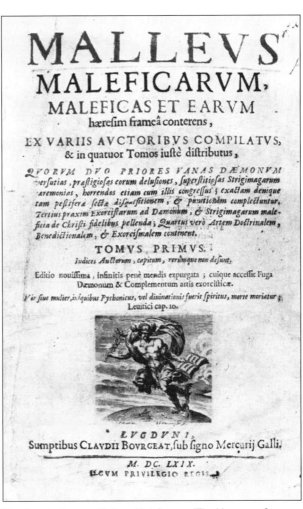

The frontispiece to *Malleus Maleficarum* (*The Hammer of Witches*), the 1486 book that served as the major reference manual on witches for two centuries.

about the subject, they could consult *Maelleus Maleficarum* ("Hammer of the Witches"), written in 1486 by a group of German monks. For two hundred years *Maelleus Maleficarum* was the second most popular book in the world, right after the Bible. Judges presiding over witchcraft trials in Europe kept a pocket-size edition of it by their sides to consult as they sent thousands of people to their deaths. Nearer to home, a prominent Boston minister named Increase Mather had written a book in 1684 entitled *An Essay for the Recording of Illustrious Providences*, or *Remarkable Providences*, which included detailed accounts of a supposed episode of witchcraft that had taken place in the nearby town of Groton in 1671.

It was believed that a witch was a person who entered into a pact with the devil in exchange for supernatural powers to do evil. The evil acts—the *maleficia*—of witches included wicked deeds such as damaging crops, making the milk curdle, and causing illness or death to people and animals.

Beyond any immediate harm witches were thought to cause, their most serious crime was that of recruiting people to sign the book of Satan and join the ranks of his evil minions.

A drawing depicting three witches standing around a boiling cauldron; above them hovers the devil.

THE CITY ON A HILL

If Satan was trying to bring the inhabitants of Massachusetts into his fold, he was attempting the spiritual seduction of an exceptional group of people with an exalted sense of their destiny. The English villages of Massachusetts had been settled beginning in the early 1600s by a Protestant sect called the Puritans. In theology, the Puritans were Calvinists, believing that the vast majority of human beings were sinners doomed to suffer eternal hellfire, that a very small group of "the elect" would be saved, and that God, knowing everything, already knew who the saved would turn out to be. Naturally, most of the saved would be Calvinists.

The Puritans dressed plainly in black and white and wore their hair simply, in contrast to the lacy collars, brilliant cloth, and curly wigs that were then fashionable in Europe. They shunned music and dancing. They made a point of working on Christmas, which they considered to be a pagan holiday. They hoped to show by their austere ways that they were worthy of salvation.

The government of King Charles I considered the Puritans dangerous, for they opposed the Church of England, the religion of the state and of the monarch. Charles encouraged them to go to the colonies. The Puritans were eager to go, inspired by the idea of starting a new society far from the temptations of Europe. The settlers' leader, John Winthrop, gave words to this sense of mission, and in so doing he created a myth of American destiny that has persisted until the present day. The new colony, said Winthrop, would be "a city upon a hill," and "the eyes of all people" would be on them. Though most Americans are not descended from the Puritans, the character of the United States owes a great deal to them. They were tough, thrifty, hard-working pioneers who brought with them England's most democratic institutions. These institutions formed the basis of democracy when the colonies became a nation.

The American sense of destiny has also persisted. Long after the Puritans, with their buckled shoes and punishments for Sabbath-breaking, had faded into a quaint legend, Americans would continue to be drawn to the idea that their country has a mission—as an example of human liberty, as a promised land for immigrants.

TROUBLE IN SALEM

In Salem, people had been seeing signs of the devil's presence even before the strange behavior of the girls in Samuel Parris's household announced it to them. A succession of Indian raids and smallpox epidemics made the settlers feel as though their world could fall apart at any time. The political security of Salem was in jeopardy as well: Massachusetts had been in legal limbo ever since the charter giving the colony the right to govern itself had been revoked by the British

Crown eight years earlier. All attempts to negotiate a new charter had failed, and the inhabitants of this small farming community were growing anxious about their rights to the land they had worked so hard and long to cultivate.

There was also tension in the community between old settlers and new settlers, between the town of Salem, which was located on the coast, and the village of Salem, which was located inland. Salem Town, part of the seaboard world of merchants and mariners, was relatively worldly and freethinking. Salem Village, which had been created to provide food for Salem Town, was inhabited by more traditional Puritans, who disliked the individualism they saw emerging in Salem Town. The leaders in Salem Village wanted to distance themselves, legally, from Salem Town's corrupting influences. As a first step, they founded a separate church for the village and invited Samuel Parris (father of the bewitched Betty) to be its minister. These conflicts would take a dark turn when both these rival factions began to suspect that their enemies were the allies of Satan.

THE FIRST ACCUSATIONS

As the girls, Betty and Abigail, continued to behave more and more strangely, Samuel Parris called in ministers from neighboring towns and villages to look at them. The ministers all agreed that the children were bewitched—that is, they were victims of witchcraft. In the ministers' view, the bewitchment of the girls explained many things. Clearly, Satan had allies in Salem doing his bidding. Indian attacks, the lack of a charter from England, the strife between town and village, the smallpox outbreaks, even the bitterness of the winter: it was all Satan's work.

Word of the bewitchment spread, and people came to see the amazing antics of the afflicted girls. They watched as Betty and Abigail jumped under tables and twisted their bodies into seemingly impossible positions. When the villagers asked the girls who was hurting them, the girls refused to answer.

Finally, Mary Sibley, one of the women of Salem, decided to take matters into her own hands. It was known that witches usually had evil helpers known as familiars—devils who would disguise themselves as dogs, cats, or birds, or any weird combination of animals. (A familiar of one of the accused Salem witches, for example, was "a thing with a head like a woman with two leggs and wings.") Mary Sibley suspected the Parrises' dog of being a familiar. Hoping to break the evil spell, she made use of an old white-magic remedy. Under Sibley's direction, the Parrises' slave, Tituba, baked a "witch cake" out of flour and Betty's and Abigail's urine and fed it to the dog.

When Samuel Parris found out about the witch cake, he was furious. As far as he was concerned, there was no such thing as good magic. It was all the work of the devil, and using it was tantamount to "[going] to the Devil for help against the Devil," he said. During religious services, the minister raged, "The Devil hath been raised among us and his rage is vehement and terrible, and, when he shall be silenced, the Lord only knows."

Parris seemed to have a point, for after the baking of the witch cake, two more girls announced that they were afflicted. One of them was Anne Putnam, Jr., the twelve-year-old daughter of Thomas and Ann Carr Putnam.

At last, four days after the baking of the witch cake, the girls named their tormentors: Sarah Osborne, Sarah Good, and Tituba.

Painting showing Puritans on their way to church, by George Henry Boughton, 1867.

Sarah Osborne was a sick, penniless old woman. Sarah Good was a homeless beggar. In their lowly condition, both women resembled the many thousands who had been executed as witches in Europe in the previous two centuries.

Tituba was a Native American slave Samuel Parris had brought over with him from Barbados. During the long winter, Betty and Abigail had spent a lot of time with Tituba, who entertained them with tales of magic and sorcery. One of the things the girls liked to do with Tituba was play at fortunetelling. They would drop the white of an egg into a glass of water. Whatever form the egg white took would indicate the profession of their future sweethearts. During one of the girls' séances, the egg white turned into the shape of a coffin. John Hale, a pastor in a neighboring town, would later write that the coffin was "a just warning to others to take heed of handling the Devil's weapons."

It was soon after the incident with the egg-white coffin in mid-January that the girls began to show symptoms of their mysterious disease. By the end of the following month, they had made their first accusations of witchcraft. The witch-hunt had begun.

THE MAGISTRATES MARCH INTO TOWN

In 1692, English legal procedures were far less systematic and fair than they would later become, and in the colonies they were even more irregular. There was no police force; officials called "magistrates" performed the roles of judges. Magistrates were usually men of high standing in the community, but they did not necessarily have any legal training.

In criminal trials, the accused were not represented by defense counsel. There was no one responsible for protecting their rights. Defendants were not considered innocent until proven guilty, and torture was widely used to extract confessions. Modern ideas about the rights of the accused, rights ultimately written into the U.S. Constitution, were still undergoing development in England.

Thomas Putnam, the most prominent landowner in the village and the father of the most "afflicted" of the afflicted girls, asked the town's magistrates to investigate the crime. Accompanied by marshals armed with spears, they rode in from Salem Town to examine the suspects. Crowds from Salem and the surrounding villages flocked to the meetinghouse, where the hearings were held. The witch-hunt had now become an official legal proceeding.

THE QUESTIONING BEGINS

Presiding over the hearings were two magistrates from Salem Town, Jonathan Corwin and John Hathorne. Hathorne was the great-grandfather of Nathaniel Hawthorne, who would one day write about his Puritan ancestors in the novel *The Scarlet Letter*.

A late-fifteenth-century woodcut depicting three witches assuming the forms of strange-looking animals as they fly through the air.

The first person brought in to be examined was Sarah Good. Pregnant and dressed in rags, Sarah Good persisted in proclaiming her innocence. Every time she denied the charges, the afflicted girls would fall into hysterics. Throughout the months of proceedings, the girls would, as a matter of routine, have fits whenever one of the alleged witches took the witness stand. A glance from a witch was thought to be capable of inflicting physical pain on her victim. To protect the girls, the magistrates directed the accused to keep their gazes averted from the girls at all times. Once, on her way to be questioned, an accused witch glanced across the square toward the meeting-house, apparently causing a heavy roof beam inside to come crashing to the floor.

"Sarah Good," Magistrate Hathorne asked, "do you not see now what you have done? Why do you not tell us the truth? Why do you thus torment these poor children?"

"I do not torment them."

"Who do you employ then?" Hathorne pressed.

"I employ nobody. I scorn it."

"How came they thus tormented?"

"What do I know?"

At this point in the questioning, Good made an effort to turn the attentions of the magistrates away from herself and toward another scapegoat.

"You bring others here and now you charge me with it," she said.

"Why, who was it?" asked Hathorne, goading the frightened woman.

"I do not know but it was some you brought into the meetinghouse with you."

Tituba teaching witchcraft to four children.

"We brought you into the meetinghouse."

"But you brought two more."

"Who was it then, that tormented the children?"

"It was Osborne," said Sarah Good.

Sarah Osborne was questioned next. Osborne, who had been dragged out of her sickbed to stand before the magistrates, said she was "more like to be be-witched than she was a witch." At one point she made a feeble attempt to join the ranks of the afflicted, complaining about having been pinched by invisible forces, all the while steadfastly refusing to admit to being a witch. But her pathetic ploy did not work, and she was dragged off to jail, where she would later die, the first victim of the Salem witch-hunt.

TITUBA'S CONFESSION

Last to be called before the magistrates was Tituba, who admitted very early in the questioning that she was, indeed, a witch. Having been beaten by Parris into confessing, she now stood before the magistrates and a packed house of villagers and shocked everyone with fantastic stories about flying around the village on broomsticks and being visited by strange creatures, sometimes in the form of a beast like a hog or a "great dog."

Tituba's confession marked the end of the first phase of the outbreak. A witch had confessed! Soon everyone would be wondering who among them were witches or wizards. In the months to come neighbor would turn against neighbor; husband would turn against wife; and child would turn against parent.

Confessing to witchcraft was the only way that an accused witch was able to escape execution, and soon the accused realized that it was safer for them to confess than it was for them to maintain their innocence.

In order to make their confessions more believable, the accused witches wove elaborate tales of their bewitchments, telling how they had come face-to-face with the devil, who sometimes appeared in the form of a black man with a hat, and how they had been forced to sign his book with their own blood. They told how they had attended witches' covens where they were given red bread to eat and red wine to drink and heard witches discuss "pulling down the Kingdom of Christ and setting up the Kingdom of Satan."

Prodded on by the judges, the accused charged other members of the community of witchcraft and soon the line between the accuser and the accused became blurred.

By the end of the witch scare 55 of the more than 160 people accused of witchcraft would confess. Each confession would be bolstered by more accusations and eventually the ranks of the "afflicted" grew to nineteen, most of them female, most of them young girls. The escalating confessions and accusations reinforced people's fear that the devil was taking over the community.

MORE ACCUSATIONS

The witch-hunt gained momentum in March, when Anne Putnam, Jr., accused Martha Cory, a respectable church member, of bewitching her. The idea that the devil had managed to infiltrate the ranks of admired members of the community made it seem as though the village were infested with witches.

Martha Cory's open skepticism about the hearings had made her vulnerable to attack. Her response to being accused of witchcraft was "Nay, we must not believe these distracted children."

A week later Rebecca Nurse, a woman revered by all, was accused by several of the girls. On the same day that Rebecca Nurse was brought in to be examined, Dorcas Good, the four-year-old daughter of Sarah Good, was questioned, as part of the investigation into the guilt of her mother. Dorcas said that she "had a Snake that used to Suck on the lowest Joynt of [her] for-finger." Upon examining her finger, the magistrates detected a red spot (most likely a flea bite). As far as the magistrates were concerned, this was proof that Dorcas was suckling a demon. At the end of the day, the four-year-old child and the saintly old Rebecca Nurse were sent to jail.

By the end of May, there were at least thirty-nine people in jail.

IN THE JAILS OF SALEM

Illustration created by Howard Pyle for an article ("The Second Generation of Englishmen in America," *Harpers New Monthly Magazine,* 1883), depicting an old hag being arrested for witchcraft.

The proceedings that had taken place so far were all preliminary hearings. Without a charter, the colony could not legally hold trials, and so the accused were made to languish for months in filthy, rat-infested prisons, which were unbearably cold in the winter and unbearably hot in the summer.

Beyond being forced to endure the inhumane treatment of and daily indignities of life in the miserable prisons, the witches were systematically tortured in an attempt to extract confessions from them. They were made to stand in one position for hours of brutal interrogation. Their necks were tied to their heels until blood gushed out of their noses. They suffered from not knowing what had become of their children, many of whom were left with no one to care for them. Although most of the accused were women, as time wore on more and more men were accused as well, and the streets of Salem were scattered with abandoned children who had not only lost their parents but also their homes, since the property of all accused witches was seized.

A local merchant described what had become of the belongings of one of the supposed witches: "The sheriff came to his house and seized all the goods, provisions and cattle that he could come at . . . threw out the beer of the barrel, and carried away the barrel; emptied a pot of broth, and took away the pot, and left nothing in the house for the support of the children."

THE COURT OF OYER AND TERMINER

Finally, on May 14, Massachusetts was granted its long-awaited charter. Along with the new charter, the colony received a new governor, William Phips. Phips set up a Court of *Oyer* and *Terminer* ("to hear" and "to determine" in French legal language). Courts of Oyer and Terminer were special courts that could be convened by colonial governors in the absence of regular courts of justice. Phips appointed nine magistrates to be judges and twelve people to serve on the jury. At the same time, he ordered the alleged witches to be put into chains.

To the twenty-first-century mind, one of the strangest things about the Salem

Illustration (originally appearing in *Pioneers in the Settlement of America* by William A. Crafts) depicting a courtroom scene in which an "afflicted" girl falls on the floor as an accused woman stands holding her right hand over her heart and gesturing upward as if declaring her innocence.

witch trials was the nature of the evidence that the judges considered acceptable in a court of law. According to *Maelleus Maleficarum,* the standard reference manual on witchcraft at the time, a telltale sign that a person was a witch was the presence on her body of a "witch's teat." A witch's teat was thought to serve the same function as the nipple of a nursing mother, but instead of providing milk to babies, it supplied blood to the witch's evil helpers, or familiars. A committee of physicians searched the bodies of the accused. Any imperfection in the skin—a wart, a pimple, a mole, a birthmark, a freckle—was deemed to be evidence of the specially adapted teat the witch used to suckle her familiars. "A preternatural excrescence of flesh" thought to be the dreaded teat was discovered in the genital areas of three of the accused women.

But the strangest evidence of all was the afflicted girls' assertions that they had seen apparitions of the witches—either in the appearance of the witches themselves or in the form of their familiars. Throughout the trials, the girls told frightening and increasingly elaborate tales of being visited by the "spectres" of the accused witches. It was thought that witches allowed the devil to appear in their forms in order to inflict harm on his victims. The spectral shapes of the witches were visible only to the afflicted. Many people were sent to their deaths on no firmer basis than this so-called spectral evidence.

THE EXECUTIONS BEGIN

The first witch to be executed was Bridget Bishop, a tavern keeper who had been previously accused (and subsequently exonerated) of witchcraft. One of the villagers, Samuel Gray, testified that Bishop's specter had appeared over the cradle of his child, who shortly thereafter fell ill and died.

In response to Hathorne's questioning, Bishop said, "I am innocent to a witch. I know not what a witch is."

Hathorne rejoined, logically and cruelly, "How do you know then that you are not a witch?"

On June 10, 1692, Bishop was taken in a cart up to the first hill to be found on

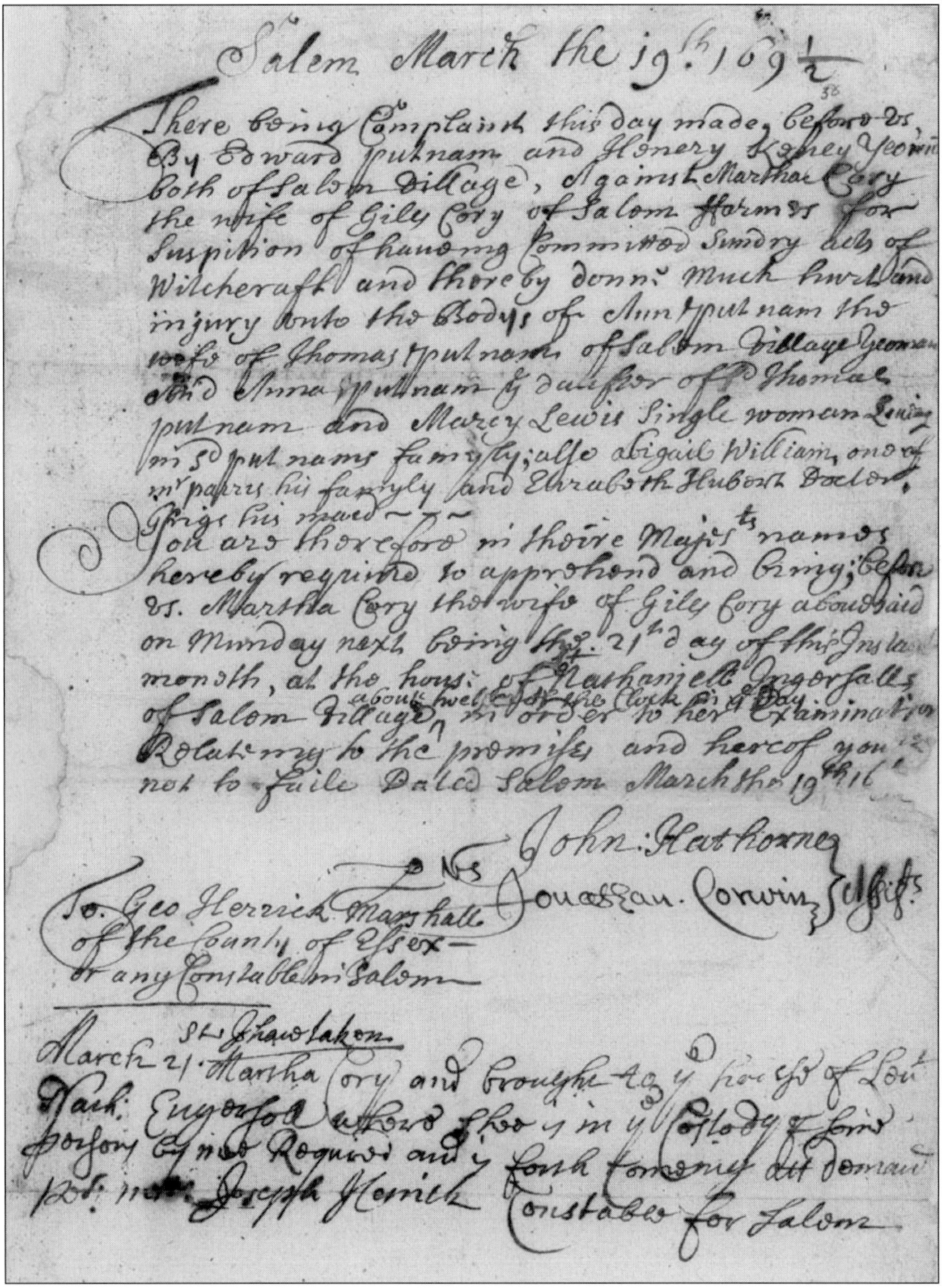

A copy of the original warrant for the arrest of Martha Cory.

the way out of Salem, a barren rock elevation that came to be known as Gallows Hill, and there she was hanged in front of a crowd of jeering onlookers. To save the trouble of burying her body, it was thrown into the crevices between the rocks. This is how the eighteen other bodies that would be hanged on Gallows Hill would be disposed of as well.

When Bishop was hanged, one of the judges, Nathaniel Saltonstall, resigned in disgust. Saltonstall, who would later be accused of being a witch, although never arrested, was the first of a small core of prominent officials who had the courage to speak out against the trials.

In the wake of Bridget Bishop's hanging, a group of Boston ministers wrote to the governor, urging that caution be used in the prosecution of the witches. What resulted was a document entitled *The Return of the Several Ministers Consulted*. The message conveyed by *The Return* was a mixed one: while saying that "exceeding tenderness" should be used toward the accused, the document gave a closing recommendation for a "speedy and vigorous prosecution" of the witches, thus undermining its ability to act as a force of moderation.

The contagion continued to spread, extending beyond Salem to the surrounding towns of Andover, Ipswich, Gloucester, and other outlying areas. When the court reconvened on June 29, five more accused witches were tried. Among them was Rebecca Nurse, who would be the sole person to be acquitted, but only very briefly. The jury's verdict of not guilty for Nurse sent the girls into an agony of fits. In response, Chief Justice William Stoughton urged the members of the jury to reconsider, and they eventually came back with the sought-after guilty verdict.

There was a lot of unease surrounding Nurse's conviction. Thirty-nine people had signed a petition on her behalf. Her daughter, Sarah Nurse, had cast doubt on the girls' credibility with a deposition in which she stated: "I saw Goody Bibber pull pins out of her close [*sic*] and held them between her fingers and clasped her hands round her knees and then she cried out and said Goody Nurse pinched her. This I can testify."

But the girls and Stoughton prevailed. The jury caved in and now Rebecca Nurse would be executed.

It was dangerous to doubt the accusers, but there were always some who were willing to take the risk for the sake of standing up for what they believed. John Proctor, a sixty-year-old farmer and tavern owner from Salem Town, asserted that the behavior of the afflicted girls could be corrected with harsh discipline, saying, "If they were let alone so we should all be Devils & witches quickly." Soon after making that statement, Proctor would be executed for the crime of witchcraft.

On July 19, five witches were hanged. In response to Reverend Nicholas Noyes's request that she confess as she mounted the scaffold, Sarah Good shot back, "I am no more a witch than you are a wizard, and if you take away my life, God will give you blood to drink." (Ironically, years later, Noyes would suffer an internal hemorrhage and end up choking to death on his own blood.)

On August 5, there were six more convictions. Among those found guilty was George Burroughs, a former minister of Salem Village who gave a moving recita-

This mid-nineteenth-century painting, *Examination of a Witch* by Thompkins H. Matteson, depicts a young girl being stripped and examined for "witch marks."

tion of the Lord's Prayer at his hanging. Witches were supposed to be incapable of prayer, and Burroughs's perfect rendition made many of the villagers have second thoughts about what was happening. At one point it looked as if some of the spectators would try to stop the execution. To quell the crowd, Cotton Mather, the son of Increase Mather (author of *Remarkable Providences*) and the best-known New England Puritan minister of his generation, proclaimed that the devil was known to transform himself "into an angel of light."

Most of the accused submitted to the trials. There was, however, one exception: Giles Cory, the husband of Martha

This painting, created by Thomas Slatterwhite Noble in 1869, depicts a condemned woman being marched to Gallows Hill.

Cory, who had already been accused of witchcraft. Giles Cory was an irascible eighty-year-old landowner, and he refused to be tried. Pointing out that no one called before the Court of Oyer and Terminer was ever let off, he said that he "rather chose to undergo what death they would put him to."

Resorting to an Old English form of torture known as *peine forte et dure*, the magistrates ordered that Cory be forced to lie naked on the ground, his hands and legs bound, while a succession of heavy rocks was piled upon his chest. With each rock heaped onto him, the magistrates would command Cory to confess, but throughout the course of the two days that it took him to die, Cory never wavered in his contempt for the proceedings. According to some reports, his only reply to the magistrates was "More weight, more weight."

THE END OF THE TRIALS

In early September six more of the accused witches were hanged. That would be the last set of hangings.

The events of the previous months had created a feeling of general unrest among the people of Salem. The execution of the saintly Rebecca Nurse, the moving recitation of the Lord's Prayer by George Burroughs before his death, the stubborn heroism of old Giles Cory, all combined to sow the seeds of doubt in the minds of many of the villagers.

Finally that unrest manifested itself in doubts about the afflicted girls themselves. The girls started overreaching themselves: the people they cried out against were more and more prominent. Things started to backfire on them when they included in their list of the accused Lady Phips, the wife of Governor Phips.

There was no one point at which it can be said that the madness of Salem was at an end, but looking back from this distance, it is easy enough to read the signs that indicated it was. In October, Phips wrote to London. After blaming the trials on the "loud cries and clamours" of the people, he went on to express his misgivings about them: "I found that the Devill had taken upon him the name and shape of severall persons who were doubtless innocent and to my certain knowledge of good reputation for which cause I have now forbidden the committing of any more that shall be accused without unavoidable necessity." At a witch trial of twenty-six people in January 1693, all but three who had confessed were found not guilty, and Phips later pardoned the three who had been found guilty. (In 1694, Phips was recalled to London, where he died shortly after his arrival.)

One day, the afflicted girls went to investigate an incident of witchcraft in a neighboring town. Encountering an old woman along the way, the girls proceeded to go into one of their fits. But instead of turning on the woman, the people passing by simply told the constable who accompanied them to take the "wenches" elsewhere. Recovering their composure, the girls returned home. After that, they made no more accusations.

Ironically, a book written by one of the witch-hunt's most prominent advocates ultimately helped to end it. In *Cases of Conscience*, Increase Mather, father of Cotton, argued forcefully against the use of spectral evidence, pointing out that casting suspicion on good people might be one of the devil's tricks: "To take away the life of anyone, merely because a specter or Devil, in a bewitched or possessed person does accuse them, will bring the guilt of innocent blood on the land."

After making his statement, Mather interviewed

This illustration, which appeared in *Frank Leslie's Weekly* (a literary and news magazine founded in 1852), depicts Reverend George Burroughs standing with his hands in chains at his trial for witchcraft. The original *Leslie's* caption read: "The legend of Salem: The Rev. George Burroughs was accused of witchcraft on the evidence of feats of strength, tried, hung, and buried beneath the gallows."

confessors in prison, the majority of whom recanted. Eight of the confessors told him that they had forsworn themselves to please the judges, whom they feared, and to prolong their lives. In a deposition, Sarah Ingersoll, the innkeeper of the tavern in which the trials were held, wrote how one of the accused girls told her how she was coerced into confessing: "She came to me crying and wringing her hands, seemingly to be much troubled in spirit. I asked her what she ailed. She answered, she had outdone herself." The girl told Ingersoll that "if she told Mr. Noyes but once [that] she had set her hand to the Book [witches' book] he would leave her [alone], but, if she told him the truth, and said she had not set her hand to the book, a hundred times he would not believe her."

"It was all false," one of the other girls stated.

THE AFTERMATH

Within two years of the end of the witch trials, the colony of Massachusetts abolished witchcraft as a crime. On January 15, 1697, it held a Day of Humiliation during which one judge and all twelve Salem jurors begged forgiveness. In a written statement, the jurors admitted, "We ourselves were not capable to understand, nor able to withstand the mysterious delusions of the Power of Darkness, and the Prince of the Air [i.e., Satan]."

Portrait of Cotton Mather, a prominent Puritan minister, who played an important role in fanning the flames of the witch hysteria in Salem, Massachusetts, in 1692.

The year 1697 also saw the death of John Hale, a minister who had favored the witch trials until his wife was accused. Before he died, Hale wrote a book, the title beginning, *A Modest Enquiry into the Nature of Witchcraft . . .* Published in 1702, the book concluded that the trials had been based on "unsafe principles." "Such was the darkness of that day, the tortures and lamentations of the afflicted, and the power of former presidents [precedents] that we walked in the clouds, and could not see our way."

Samuel Parris was eventually forced to leave Salem. William Stoughton, who was the chief judge at the trials as well as the colony's lieutenant governor, never apologized for his actions and eventually became governor of Massachusetts. Cotton Mather, who had talked a crowd out of preventing the execution of George Burroughs, later achieved fame for his eloquent sermons and writings. Before he died in 1728, he lent his voice to the cause of smallpox vaccination—a medical advance that would one day lead to the eradication of the disease. It is difficult to draw one moral from so mixed a record; perhaps the point Cotton Mather's life best illustrates is that people are neither wholly good nor wholly evil.

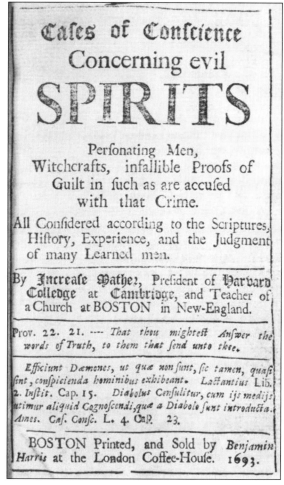

The title page of the 1693 edition of *Cases of Conscience Concerning Evil Spirits* by Increase Mather.

In 1706, Ann Putnam, Jr.—who at the height of the witch scare had claimed to have been bewitched by a total of seventeen of the accused—made a public confession in Salem's church. She asked to "be humbled before God for that sad and humbling providence" that led, in 1692, to her becoming "an instrument for the accusing of several persons of a grievous crime, whereby their lives were taken away." She died, unmarried, in May 1715.

Of the other afflicted girls, some were married and had children, some did not marry, some lived long lives, some died within a few years of the trials, and others simply walked out of the spotlight of history, their fate forever unknown.

"These aliens, driven out of Germany and Bohemia
for treasonable teachings by Bismarck and the Emperor
of Austria, have swarmed into this country of extreme toleration
and have flagrantly abused its hospitality."
—Chicago Tribune, *May 8, 1886*

"The city went insane."
—Mother Jones (nickname for
the labor organizer Mary Harris Jones)

A *Harper's Weekly* illustration of the police being caught in the explosion.

✤ *Chapter 2* ✤
The Haymarket Bomb Trial

On the night of May 4, 1886, Chicago police were getting ready to break up a meeting of industrial workers in a place called Haymarket Square when someone threw a bomb. The event led to the deaths of seven policemen and provided America with a new devil—the anarchist, "a fiend with a smoking gun and a bomb."

ARE YOU AN ANARCHIST?

Immigrants arriving on New York's Ellis Island at the beginning of the twentieth century had to go through rigorous inspections before they were allowed to enter the country. Doctors examined them for signs of mental handicap or disease. Each newcomer had to answer a series of questions designed to weed out undesirables: "Can you read and write? Have you been in a prison, almshouse, or an institution for the care of the insane?" There was one political question: "Are you an anarchist?"

If the answer was yes, the immigrant was sent back to the Old World on the next boat, along with the people who had tuberculosis or typhus. Like them, he was thought to carry a dangerous contagion. He was infected with a political disease that caused assassinations and bombings.

"WILD-EYED FIEND"

For a fifty-year period, between 1880 and 1930, the word *anarchist* could send a shiver of fear up the spines of stockbrokers in silk hats, kings in braided uniforms, and ordinary newspaper-reading citizens in America and in Europe. For most people, the word conjured up the image of "a wild-eyed fiend, armed with a smoking revolver and a bomb" (so the historian Henry David summarized the typical American's idea of the anarchist).

In their fiery writings and speeches, anarchists called for a mighty uprising that would change the world forever. It would begin with a strike of all workers: laborers would put down their tools, leave the factories, and abandon the controls of the trains and streetcars they drove, bringing the economy to a halt and the

PUT THEM OUT AND KEEP THEM OUT ·Copyright, 1919, by The Philadelphia Inquirer Co

Cartoon depicting Communism and anarchy creeping under the American flag, 1919, by Fred Morgan.

ruling classes to their knees. The chain of events unleashed by this great strike would, anarchists believed, bring an end to poverty. Property, government, and class distinctions would disappear, giving way to the reign of perfect freedom, equality, and justice.

Anarchism had much in common with socialism, the other radical political response to the vast upheavals of the Industrial Revolution, and the general public had a hard time telling the two movements apart. One important difference, though, was that anarchists killed people. In the years before the First World War, six heads of state were killed by men calling themselves anarchists.

But anarchists did not limit their attacks to kings and politicians. Convinced that their cause justified any action, throughout the 1880s and 1890s anarchists threw bombs at people marching in parades, celebrating a monarch's birthday, or just sitting in cafés listening to music. Though the damage done and the number of people hurt were minimal by today's standards, these attacks had an enormous impact. Terrorism was a new idea then. Dynamite, which had been invented only in 1867, for the first time put a weapon of mass destruction into the hands of anyone with a little ingenuity and a lot of deadly intent.

What could motivate people to commit these seemingly senseless crimes? For the police, politicians, and editors of the most widely read newspapers in the United States, the answer was simple—anarchism was a political disease that had invaded America from Europe, where the powerless poor were numerous. America was a democratic country where anyone could rise through hard work; it could never have spawned an ideology like anarchism. Some of the richest men in the United States had started with nothing. If the United States had an anarchist movement—and indeed, it had one of the largest in the world—then this was an unfortunate side effect of immigration. Along with the honest people looking for a better life, some insane fanatics had managed to get in.

This explanation seemed reasonable, because many of America's radicals were immigrants. But it failed to take into account a host of other facts. The Industrial Revolution that had begun in Europe was now sweeping the United States at an astonishing pace. Industry was reshaping society—welding the continent together with railways and telegraph lines; mass-producing cheap shoes and canned meat, hair cream and sewing machines; and erecting great cities complete with gas lamps, streetcars, and elevated trains. A byproduct of all this industrialization was a drastic change in the ground rules of American life: it was creating a handful of fantastically wealthy captains of industry and millions of desperate people who had nothing to lose.

THE BOMB IN HAYMARKET SQUARE

The most famous anarchist bombing of the nineteenth century took place in Chicago on May 4, 1886, and it arose out of the bitter labor conflicts that had plagued the city for twenty years. The day before the bombing, police had fired into a crowd of factory workers on strike, killing as many as four of them. To protest the shooting, a rally was held the next night near a place called Haymarket Square. The crowd was already dispersing when a police chief inspector known for his eagerness to deal harshly with strikers dispatched his men to hasten the breakup of the meeting. As the police marched into the crowd, someone threw a bomb into their ranks. The police responded with wild pistol fire. Seven policemen ultimately died from their wounds.

The Haymarket bombing led to the trial of eight anarchists: August Spies, a furniture maker; Michael Schwab, a bookbinder; Samuel Fielden, a stone hauler; Adolph Fischer, a typesetter; Oscar Neebe, a former ship's cook; Louis Lingg, a carpenter; George Engel, a wagon maker; and Albert Parsons, a newspaper compositor and former Confederate soldier.

The courtroom battle that followed was closely watched throughout the United States and Europe. Looking back on it today, we can see that the Haymarket bomb trial was a trial of the American judicial system as it existed in the 1880s as much as it was a trial of the men accused of the bombing. It tested the court's ability to deal fairly with a group of defendants who frightened and enraged almost the whole society. It tested the court's ability to put what it considered to be the devil on trial.

In the Chicago stockyards. Chicago was the center of the American meatpacking industry in the 1880s. Note the Armour packing plant in the background.

A "PILING UP OF BLIND FORCES"

Although an incident like the Haymarket bombing could have occurred in any major manufacturing city in the United States, it was not surprising that it occurred in Chicago, the fastest-growing big city in the country, with the bitterest labor conflicts, the toughest factory owners, and the angriest and most outspoken work force.

Chicago exhibited all the light and darkness, all the energy and brutality, of the new industrial America. "Murderously actual" was how the architect Frank Lloyd Wright described the city—a "piling up of blind forces." All the railroads

Workers entering McCormick Reaper Works in the 1880s. Police shot several striking workers here on the day before the Haymarket bombing.

of the West led to Chicago. It was to Chicago that the hogs and cattle were brought to be processed in the city's meatpacking plants; and it was from Chicago that they were shipped off the next day as chops, steaks, and rib racks in refrigerator cars that had been manufactured in Chicago. Chicago's mail-order companies supplied the nation's farmers and their families with everything from whalebone corsets to prefabricated houses. The factories of the McCormick Reaper Works in Chicago poured out the harvesting machines that were stitching the prairie into even squares of quilted cornfields and wheat fields. For tourists coming to the United States in the late 1800s, Chicago was an attraction equal to Niagara Falls.

But as it turned hogs into hams, lumber into furniture, and molten metal into reaping machines, Chicago was also busy manufacturing a new brand of misery. More than half the city's workers were immigrants who had been drawn to the metropolis by the promise of (relatively) high-paying jobs. And though there were certainly plenty of jobs in Chicago, there were many more workers than jobs. Wages went up and down with the fluctuations of the economy, making workers' lives uncertain and confronting many of them with a deprivation greater than anything they had ever known in the Old World. Workers lived in rooming houses, crowded together in the homes of relatives, or in cheaply built shanties located near open sewers and unpaved streets. Many simply camped out. In 1870, a prosperous year for the city, there were twenty thousand homeless workers wandering the streets by day and sleeping in alleys and under bridges in the dead of winter.

American workers had no safety net in those days. There was no such thing as minimum wage, unemployment insurance, workmen's compensation, social security, or welfare. When business was slow, factories lowered wages or simply fired workers, leaving them with nothing but charity to fall back on. Charity was not always available—charity was supposed to be bad for workers' characters—so unemployment in those years meant more than an inability to pay for any of the specialty goods displayed in Chicago's shop windows. It meant hunger for the worker and his family.

A child laborer linking bedding springs in a factory in Boston, Massachusetts.

Even in boom times, some workers did not earn enough to support themselves, and it often fell on children to supplement the family income by working in factories, peddling newspapers, shining shoes, sewing buttons, making artificial flowers, or rolling the fat cigars that, in those days, were always burning in the mouths of successful men.

Occasionally politicians attempted to improve labor conditions by proposing legislation to regulate wages or shift lengths (which in the 1880s commonly ran ten or eleven hours, sometimes as long as fourteen). Factory owners considered all such efforts to be a misguided interference with the laws of the economy, which would just make workers lazy. As the creators of the country's new wealth, business leaders had little trouble seeing to it that their views prevailed.

THE LABOR MOVEMENT

In the 1820s workers in the United States and Europe began to organize themselves into labor unions. Through labor unions, workers found strength in numbers. For the first time in their lives, they had the ability to bargain for higher wages and better working conditions: unions gave workers the power to threaten bosses with their most effective weapon, the labor strike. All at once, they could lay down their tools and bring the factory to a halt, immediately cutting into their employers' profits, damage that got worse every minute goods weren't produced and customers' orders weren't filled. Larger industry-wide strikes could have even more powerful effects. A strike of streetcar workers could stop a city. A strike of railroad workers could stall the entire U.S. economy, as essential products and resources couldn't get to the next city.

If things went as strikers intended, they would resume work when their demands had been met or some compromise had been reached. Factory owners were extremely reluctant to permit such an outcome. In fact, most of them considered union demands to be a complicated form of robbery, and at first judges were inclined to agree. At the behest of business, judges issued court orders to disband the unions and force their members to pay fines. In the 1840s, when the courts ruled that unions were legal, most authorities—judges, officeholders, and police—were still on the side of the executives in labor disputes. Bosses made workers sign contracts promising, as a condition of their employment, not to join unions; they enlisted the help of other workers by paying them to act as company spies. Employers shared lists ("blacklists") of known union organizers with one another so that such men and women could not find work. But workers continued to band together anyway.

Conflicts between factory workers and bosses often turned violent. During strikes, rather than giving the workers what they were asking for in terms of higher wages or better working conditions, factory owners brought in replacements, who came to be called "strikebreakers." Strikers responded by trying to prevent strikebreakers from going to work, attacking them with fists, clubs, and stones. Employers responded by hiring armed men to escort the strikebreakers to work. The violence continued as the century wore on.

THE MOST RADICAL CITY IN THE UNITED STATES

By the mid-1880s, Chicago was the most radical city in the United States. Several thousands of its workers were anarchists, thousands more were socialists, and the majority of those who did not belong to either group joined in anarchist-led political demonstrations. Chicago's mainstream newspapers, which expressed the views of the business community, were certain that workers were drawn to extremist political ideologies only because so many of the workers were immigrants. They had brought these foreign ideas—anarchism and socialism—into this county like a contagious disease.

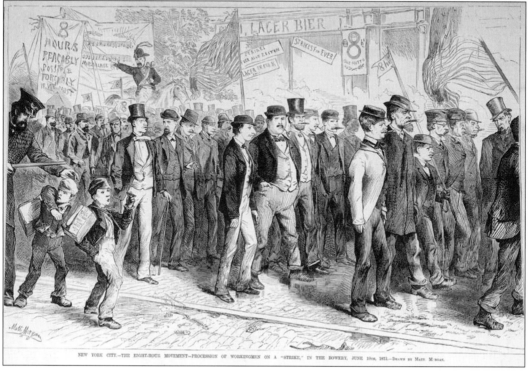

The Eight-Hour Day March as depicted in *Frank Leslie's Weekly*.

There was, however, another explanation as to why Chicago's workers were attracted to extreme solutions: American democracy had failed them. In the late 1860s, during a time of general prosperity and enthusiasm for reform in the northern United States, the Illinois legislature had passed a law establishing an official eight-hour workday, scheduled to take effect on May 1, 1867. On that day, tens of thousands of workers, including representatives from forty-four unions, marched down the city's streets carrying banners that read EIGHT HOURS AND NO CONCESSION and WE RESPECT THE LAWS OF THE STATE.

The following day, the city's largest factory owners ordered their employees to work the usual ten or eleven hours. Workers who left after eight hours were considered to be strikers, and other workers were brought in to replace them. Neither the governor nor Chicago's mayor made any effort to enforce the new law, and when strikers fought the strikebreakers, the mayor had police and militia stationed in factories and in immigrant neighborhoods in a show of force that cowed resistance—at least for the moment. Defeated, the strikers returned to their jobs.

Over the years, other clashes between Chicago workers and police created a legacy of hatred between the two groups. In 1877, during a nationwide strike in the fourth year of a depression, a total of thirty men were killed—they were all workers, and they were all killed by the Chicago police. It is not surprising, then, that many of Chicago's working people thought that the courts and the police existed mainly to serve the interests of factory owners and men of property.

THE ANARCHISTS

Nowhere was this bitter conviction—that the law and police force were on the side of the wealthy—more openly expressed than in the pages of two radical newspapers: *Arbeiter-Zeitung,* edited by a German immigrant named August Spies; and the *Alarm,* edited by a man named Albert Parsons and his wife, Lucy. Both newspapers printed fiery speeches by their editors, as well as translations of the writings of socialist thinkers Karl Marx and Freidrich Engels and anarchist thinkers Mikhail Bakunin and Jacob Most.

A native of Landeck, Germany, August Spies had come to the United States in 1872 when he was seventeen years old. After working in an upholstery shop, he took a brief stab at farming and then returned to shop work in Chicago. Handsome and well spoken, Spies embraced radical politics during the labor upheavals of the 1870s.

Albert Parsons had an unusual life story for an anarchist; indeed, the course his life had taken defied all conventional expectations. A descendant of the Pilgrims (some of his ancestors had come over on the *Mayflower*), Parsons was a former Confederate soldier. Though he had served the South during the Civil War, when the war was over Parsons embraced the cause of black emancipation. After finishing college and training as a printer, he started a newspaper called the *Spectator*, which he used to champion the rights of freedmen. In 1869, he ran for office in McLennan County, Texas, where the Ku Klux Klan was attacking blacks and "scalawags" like himself (*scalawags* was a derisive word for Southerners who sided with the North). Later, as a militiaman, he defended black voting rights. In 1872, he married an attractive dark-skinned woman named Lucy Parsons, who, according to some reports, had been born an African-American slave. Albert and Lucy Parsons were an unusual

This photo montage, created in 1887, shows five anarchists: August Spies, A. R. Parsons, Louis Lingg, George Engel, and Adolph Fischer.

couple for their time, believing in equality between the sexes as well as between blacks and whites. After their arrival in Chicago in 1874, they worked as union organizers and speakers, calling for the overthrow of the propertied classes.

MAY DAY

The Haymarket bombing, which led to the trial of August Spies, Albert Parsons, and six of Chicago's other leading anarchists, grew out of a renewed effort on the part of the labor movement to take up the fight for the eight-hour workday that had been launched in 1867. In 1886, unions across the country agreed to call for a nationwide strike, which they planned to take place on May 1, 1886.

On May 1, a total of 300,000 workers across the United States went on strike: 85,000 of those strikers lived in Chicago. Despite anarchist threats of violence (the pages of the *Alarm* suggested MAKE YOUR DEMAND FOR EIGHT HOURS WITH WEAPONS), Chicago's May Day strikes and the demonstrations that accompanied them were peaceful. But blood would be shed only a few days later, at the McCormick Reaper Works, the manufacturer of the harvesting machinery that was transforming American agriculture.

LOCKOUT

Back on February 12, 1886, the workers at McCormick Reaper Works had voted to strike. Cyrus McCormick, Jr., son of the company's founder, countered by declaring a "lockout," shutting the factory down while his managers looked for replacement workers.

Overseeing the police protection of the plant was Chief Inspector Jack Bonfield, a man with a reputation for dealing harshly with strikers. In 1885, against the orders of Chicago's mayor, Carter Harrison, Bonfield had told his men to fire their guns at a group of striking streetcar workers, a move that made him a hero to Chicago's business community.

By May, the McCormick factory was running again, with strikebreakers operating the machinery under police protection. But McCormick's labor problems were not over. Half his replacement workers had joined the strike movement. The stage was set for violence at the McCormick plant.

SHOOTING AT THE MCCORMICK PLANT

On the evening of May 3, the factory bell at McCormick Reaper Works rang out, signaling the end of the workday. When McCormick's strikebreakers started to leave the plant, the McCormick strikers charged toward the factory, planning to attack them. The police, under the command of Jack Bonfield, responded by firing into the crowd of strikers, killing as many as four workers (the exact number of those killed is unknown).

In response to this incident, Spies, who happened to have personally witnessed it, went to his newspaper office and composed a leaflet: "Workingmen, to Arms!!! Your masters sent out their bloodhounds—the police—they killed six of your brothers at McCormick's this afternoon. . . . If you are men, if you are the sons of grandsires who have shed their blood to free you, then you will rise in your might, Hercules, and destroy the hideous monster that seeks to destroy you. To arms, we call you. To arms!"

"MASS-MEETING TO-NIGHT"

In an editorial printed the next day, Spies called for workers to arm themselves. That afternoon the anarchists passed out a leaflet to announce a protest meeting to be held that night. The leaflet was printed in both English and German.

> Attention Workingmen! Great Mass-Meeting to-night, at 7:30 o'clock, at the HAYMARKET, Randolph St., Bet. Desplaines and Halsted. Good Speakers will be present to denounce the latest atrocious act of the police, the shooting of our fellow-workmen yesterday afternoon.

Twenty-five hundred people —far fewer than Spies had expected—showed up for the meeting at Haymarket Square, a place used for open-air markets in a slum neighborhood of railroad tracks, tenements, and saloons. Perhaps to avoid drawing attention to the disappointing size of the crowd, Spies moved the meeting to a space on Desplaines Street near Cranes Alley, a driveway behind a metal factory.

Chicago's Mayor Harrison, an easygoing, broad-minded politician, had also expected a larger crowd. In order to prevent a riot from taking place, he had arranged for 167 policemen to assemble at the Desplaines Street police station, half a block from Haymarket. The police were commanded by Chief Inspector Jack Bonfield, the same Jack Bonfield who had ordered the police to shoot at the workers at the McCormick plant the day before. The Haymarket meeting had been called specifically to protest these actions.

Reproduction of anarchist handbill "Attention workingmen! Great mass-meeting . . ." The same words were printed in German at the bottom of the leaflet.

Spies gave the first speech himself. Taking note of the police presence, he insisted that the meeting would be peaceable. Spies went on to call Cyrus McCormick, Jr.—who had accused him of inciting violence at the plant the day before—an "infamous liar."

"Hang him!" someone in the crowd called out.

"There will be a time, and we are rapidly approaching it, when such men as McCormick will be hanged," Spies told the crowd. "But that time has not yet come."

After Spies finished speaking, Albert Parsons addressed the crowd. Denouncing the evils of capitalism, he exhorted the workers: "Arm yourselves." Voices in the crowd shouted, "We will do it" and "We are ready now."

Believing that his presence at the scene would have a calming effect, Mayor Harrison attended the rally. He was easy enough to recognize, for he was a tall man weighing 225 pounds, well known for his big gray beard and black slouch hat. To make sure he would be noticed, he kept striking matches as though to relight his cigar. To a friend he explained, "I want the people to know their mayor is here." The speeches by Spies and Parsons left Harrison with the impression that the meeting would be peaceful. He testified later that although he would describe Parsons's speech as a "violent political harangue against capital," it was temperate compared to many other speeches he had heard on such occasions. Further, said Harrison, the crowd had remained calm and orderly, and the occasional cries of "Shoot him" or "Hang him" evoked only mild responses. In fact, several of the "Hang him" cries came from a boy standing at the edge of the crowd, and each time he shouted this, the audience would laugh.

A little before the end of Parsons's speech, Harrison left the meeting. He stopped by the police station to inform Inspector Bonfield that the meeting was "tame" and that the reinforcements could be sent home.

Mayor Carter Harrison wearing his big slouch hat.

After Parsons finished speaking, around ten o'clock, he introduced Samuel Fielden to the crowd. Fielden was an immigrant from England, the son of a Lancashire hand-loom weaver who had been active in the British labor movement. When Fielden was seven, he had gone to work in the Lancashire cotton mills, an experience he described as "satanic." After coming to America in 1868, he traveled widely. Educating himself by reading radical literature and attending socialist meetings, he became a popular speaker.

About ten minutes into Fielden's speech, a dark cloud began to approach from the north. Gusts of wind made signs creak and sent scraps of paper flying through the air. Afraid of being caught in a downpour, people began to leave. Parsons called out for the meeting to adjourn to a nearby tavern called Zepf's Hall; Parsons himself, along with fellow anarchist Adolph Fischer, went to Zepf's. Fielden, in the meantime, told the dwindling crowd of about three hundred people: "A million men hold all the property in this country. The law has no use for the other fifty-four million."

"Right enough," a voice in the crowd answered.

Fielden continued:

> You have nothing more to do with the law except to lay hands on it and throttle it until it makes its last kick. It turns your brothers out on the wayside and has degraded them until they have lost the last vestige of humanity, and they are mere things and animals. Keep your eye upon it, throttle it, kill it, stab it, do everything you can to wound it—to impede its progress.

At this point in Fielden's speech, two detectives in the crowd rushed to the Desplaines Street police station to tell Inspector Bonfield that Fielden was saying the law must be throttled and killed.

Bonfield responded by assembling his men in an alley next to the station and marching them in quick time—"almost a run"—to the rally, their ranks filling Desplaines Street from curb to curb. The buttons on their blue coats glittered in

An illustration that appeared in *Harper's Weekly* in 1886 depicting the Haymarket bombing.

the electric lights of the nearby Lyceum Theater. As they surged forward, the crowd retreated up the street and edged onto the wooden sidewalks.

Led by Inspector Bonfield and Captain William Ward, the police marched up to the speakers' wagon. "I command you, in the name of the people of the state of Illinois, immediately and peaceably to disperse!" shouted Ward.

Fielden told Ward, "But we are peaceable." When Captain Ward repeated his command, Fielden agreed to go and began to step down from the wagon.

That was when witnesses remembered hearing something sputtering over their heads, "something like a miniature rocket." Giving off a red glare, it flew about two feet in the air before falling into the middle of the street among the ranks of policemen. It lay on the ground for a few seconds before exploding with tremendous force.

Eyewitness accounts of what occurred at this point differ widely. The *Chicago Tribune* reported the next day that the blast stunned the officers, and before they could come to their senses, "the anarchists and rioters poured a shower of bullets into the police." Most of the police officers on the scene testified they had been fired at from the crowd.

The workers and speakers there that night, however, maintained that all the gunfire came from the police, and their testimony was backed by three businessmen who were at the meeting.

Everyone agreed about what happened next. "Goaded by madness," wrote the *Chicago Tribune*, "the police were in the condition of mind that permitted no resistance, and in a measure they were as dangerous as any mob of Communists, for they were blinded by passion and unable to distinguish between the peaceful citizen and Nihilist assassin." An unknown number of civilians were injured or killed by the police, at least some of them while they were attempting to flee the scene.

An illustration from *Frank Leslie's Weekly* depicts a moment after the explosion. The policemen killed in the Haymarket bombing appear on the top of the picture.

RED SCARE

As news of the event spread, fear of an anarchist uprising gripped the country. The incident had come during a time of great unrest. In 1886, more than 610,000 workers went on strike, causing Friedrich Engels, coauthor of *The Communist Manifesto,* to remark, "History is on the move over there [in the United States] at last." The bloodshed on Desplaines Street was seen by many people as a symptom of general disorder and the signal for a revolution.

White-collar workers, the middle class, and the rich united in a demand for vengeance. Newspapers around the nation fanned the fury, describing the anarchists as "cutthroats and thieves" and "monsters." Editorials compared the anarchists to animals, calling them "ungrateful hyenas," "incendiary vermin," and "slavic wolves." The *St. Louis Globe-Democrat* proclaimed, "There are no good anarchists except dead anarchists." *Harper's Weekly* described the Haymarket incident as "an outburst of anarchy, the deliberate crime of men who openly advocate massacre and the overthrow of intelligent and orderly society."

Chicago papers called for revenge. "The anarchists are amenable to no reason except that taught by the club and rifle," said the *Chicago Daily News.* The *Chicago Tribune* recommended that Congress deport anarchists and restrict immigration to keep out the "foreign savages, with their dynamite bombs." Anarchists, the *Tribune* explained, arise out of "the worst elements of the Socialistic, atheistic, alcoholic European classes."

Neither the press nor the general public seemed to appreciate the fact that the Haymarket violence had occurred within the context of other violent events—in particular, the shooting of the McCormick strikers the day before. The police reports of the incident were accepted at face value. As the labor organizer Mary Harris Jones (known as "Mother Jones") recalled in her autobiography, "The city went insane, and the newspapers did everything to keep it like a madhouse. The workers' cry for justice was drowned in the shriek for revenge."

"HE WANTED TO KEEP THE THING BOILING"

On May 5, Mayor Harrison issued a proclamation forbidding public gatherings and marches. Chicago police ransacked meeting halls, raided anarchist and socialist newspaper offices and homes, and opened mail. They rounded up hundreds of men and women without charges or warrants and beat them, partly in an attempt to extract confessions from them, but undoubtedly also for revenge.

Led by a glory-hunting police captain named Michael J. Schaack, the investigators fed newspapers' far-fetched accounts of plots

PROCLAMATION

TO THE PEOPLE OF CHICAGO:

MAYOR'S OFFICE, Chicago, May 5, 1886.

WHEREAS, Great excitement exists among the people of this good city, growing out of the LABOR TROUBLES, which excitement is intensified by the open defiance of the guardians of the peace by a body of lawless men, who, under the pretense of aiding the laboring men, are really endeavoring to destroy all law. And Whereas, last night these men, by the use of weapons never resorted to in CIVILIZED LANDS, EXCEPT IN TIMES OF WAR or for REVOLUTIONARY PURPOSES, CAUSED GREAT BLOODSHED AMONG CITIZENS AND AMONG OFFICERS of the MUNICIPALITY who were simply in the performance of their duties. And Whereas, the CITY AUTHORITIES PROPOSE TO PROTECT LIFE AND PROPERTY AT ALL HAZARDS, and in doing so will be compelled to break up all unlawful or dangerous gatherings; and

WHEREAS, Even when men propose to meet for lawful purposes, bad men will attempt to mingle with them, armed with cowardly missiles, for the purpose of bringing about bloodshed, thus endangering innocent persons;

THEREFORE, I, Carter H. Harrison, MAYOR OF THE CITY OF CHICAGO, DO HEREBY PROCLAIM THAT GATHERINGS OF PEOPLE IN CROWDS OR PROCESSIONS IN THE STREETS and PUBLIC PLACES OF THE CITY ARE DANGEROUS AND CANNOT BE PERMITTED, AND ORDERS HAVE BEEN ISSUED TO THE POLICE TO PREVENT ALL SUCH GATHERINGS and TO BREAK UP and DISPERSE ALL CROWDS, TO PREVENT INJURY TO INNOCENT PERSONS.

I urge all law-abiding people to quietly attend to their own affairs, and not to meet in crowds. If the police order any gatherings to disperse, and they be not obeyed, all persons so disobeying will be treated as law-breakers, and will surely incur the penalty of their disobedience.

I further assure the good people of Chicago that I believe the police can protect their lives and property and the good name of Chicago, and WILL do so.

CARTER H. HARRISON, Mayor.

The proclamation issued by Mayor Harrison forbidding public gatherings and marches in the wake of the Haymarket bombing.

and conspiracies. Chicago's papers accepted Schaack's stories without question and published articles that helped to convince the people of the United States that the Haymarket bomb had been the opening volley in a carefully planned anarchist insurrection. Schaack became America's best-known police detective as he and his investigators "discovered" bombs all over Chicago—most of which were nonexistent or had been planted by the police.

Schaack's superior, the chief of police Frederick Ebersold, later disclaimed responsibility for Schaack's behavior. "It was my policy to quiet matters down as soon as possible after the 4th of May. . . . On the other hand, Captain Schaack wanted to keep things stirring. . . . He wanted to keep the thing boiling."

The bombing doomed the eight-hour-workday movement. The men who had led the rally were arrested or in hiding, and the Red Scare caused by the bombing guaranteed public support for ruthless action against any workers who went on strike in support of a shorter workday.

THE POLICE FIND A SUSPECT

On May 6, in the course of a general roundup of known radicals, the police went to William Seliger's house, where they knew Louis Lingg, a young anarchist carpenter and union organizer, also resided. The police did not find Lingg, who had gone into hiding, but they did find a trunk belonging to him. Its contents included a bomb, a pistol, and a great deal of anarchist literature. Seliger was arrested, and he confessed to spending May 4 manufacturing bombs under the direction of Lingg.

Twenty-two years old, handsome, strong, and fanatical, Louis Lingg was the youngest, and the most violent, of the men who would become defendants at the trial. When he was a child in Baden, Germany, he had seen his parents destroyed by poverty. He had become an anarchist while working as a carpenter in Switzerland. When he came to the United States in 1885, he headed straight for Chicago because he knew it to be the home of a large community of anarchists. Lingg impressed other anarchists with his forceful personality and his physical courage. Nothing less than revolution would satisfy him.

After the bombing, Lingg cropped his hair, shaved his mustache, and hid out on Chicago's Southwest Side. The police got word of his whereabouts and arrested him after a violent struggle. Lingg had his hands around one detective's throat when another hit him over the head with a club.

LEGAL PROCEEDINGS BEGIN

The first policeman to succumb to injuries sustained in the Haymarket incident was Officer Mathias J. Degan. According to a coroner's inquest that was held on May 5, he had died from a wound caused by "a piece of bomb, thrown by an unknown person . . . aided, and abetted" by a list of well-known Chicago anarchists.

Less than two weeks later, on May 17, a grand jury was convened to review the results of the investigation and to determine whether a crime had been committed and if so, who should be tried for it and what the charges should be. Swept up in the mood

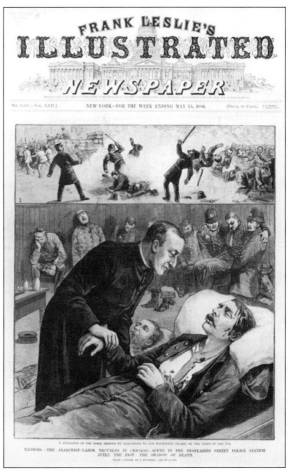

The cover of *Frank Leslie's Weekly,* May 1886. The illustration shows a priest giving last rites to a policeman.

of the time, the judge of the grand jury proceedings, John G. Rogers, instructed the jurors, "Anarchism should be suppressed." After interviewing several witnesses, the grand jury indicted ten men for the murder of Officer Degan. The accused, most of whom were associated with the anarchist newspapers the *Alarm* and *Arbeiter-Zeitung,* included Albert Parsons, the former Confederate soldier; August Spies, the German furniture maker; Samuel Fielden, the British stone hauler; Adolph Fischer, the typesetter; Louis Lingg, the young carpenter turned revolutionary; Michael Schwab, a bookbinder from Bavaria; George Engel, a fifty-year-old wagon maker from Kassel, Germany, who, like Lingg, believed the time for revolution had come; and Oscar Neebe, a former ship's cook, salesman, and factory worker who had suffered near starvation after he was fired for defending the rights of other workers at a stove factory.

Accused but never brought to trial was Rudolph Schnaubelt, a Czech machinist active in the anarchist movement, who had been seen standing near the speakers' wagon on the night of the bombing. He had been arrested and then released after several witnesses backed up his claim that he had left before the bomb exploded. After he fled the city, some police and newspapers concluded that he was the most likely person to have actually thrown the bomb. He was never caught. William Seliger, Lingg's roommate, escaped prosecution by turning state's evidence, testifying against Lingg at the trial. Except for Parsons, who was born in Texas, and Neebe, who was born in New York of German parents, all the men arrested were immigrants.

By the time of the indictment, five policemen had died of wounds received on the night of May 4. However, the anarchists were charged only with the murder of Officer Mathias Degan. Only Degan's death could be definitely attributed to the bomb and not to gunfire, which could have come as easily from the police as from the anarchists.

Considering the hysterical atmosphere at the time, the wording of the indictment was calm and reasonable. Declaring that the labor movement as a whole was not responsible for the Haymarket crime, the grand jury insisted that the idea that the eight-hour-day movement was part of a revolutionary plot was exaggerated in the public mind. Still, the grand jury believed that the Haymarket bombing was the result of "a deliberate conspiracy, the full details of which [were] in the possession of the officers of the law."

The grand jury could not see the police as fallible human beings capable of lying or distorting the truth to cover up their mistakes, nor could they see them making up tales to advance their careers, as Captain Schaack was doing. To believe such things about the police right after the Haymarket bombing would be unpatriotic; it would seem as though the jurors were indifferent to the fate of men killed in the line of duty.

DEFENDING THE DEVIL

It was difficult to find defense attorneys willing to be associated with defendants who were hated by the most powerful people in the city and viewed as less than human by millions of Americans across the country. Two of Chicago's moderate socialists formed a committee to create a fund for legal expenses, collecting money mostly by appealing to workers.

The first two lawyers willing to help were Moses Salamon and Sigmund Zeisler, neither of whom had much experience as a defense attorney. Eventually a corporate lawyer named William Black agreed to lead the team. After serving as a Union army captain in the Civil War, Black had built up a profitable law practice, which he knew he would be throwing away by leading the anarchists' defense team. (He said at the time that his actions would lead to "an almost total sacrifice of business," and in fact, most of his clients did end up abandoning him.) Black himself lacked experience as a criminal lawyer, so he asked William A. Foster, a talented criminal defense attorney who had come to Chicago from Iowa only a few months before, to join him.

William Black's keen sense of justice has won him the respect of most historians of the Haymarket affair. However, at the outset of the case, his fair-mindedness also led him to make a serious error in judgment.

Albert Parsons had gone into hiding shortly after the Haymarket bombing. Communicating with Parsons through his wife, Lucy, Black convinced the fugitive to turn himself in, thinking that in doing so Parsons would be able to show how confident he was that his innocence would be proven. Although Parsons did not agree with Black about this—he told a friend that if he surrendered he could "never expect . . . to be a free man again"—he had a weakness for dramatic gestures. On the opening day of the trial, June 21, 1886, Parsons walked into the

Photograph of a painting of the surrender of Albert Parsons to Cook County legal authorities in a crowded courtroom after he was charged with murder for his role in the Haymarket Square Riot.

courtroom. After entering a plea of not guilty, he shook hands with the other accused men and took his place among them.

A HANGING JUDGE

The panic that surrounded the Haymarket affair imperiled the defendants' chances of receiving a fair trial. To begin with, it was difficult to find jurors who had not already made up their minds about the case. Matters were made worse by the bias of the judge, Joseph E. Gary, who did not even bother trying to hide his hostility toward the accused, which in and of itself was a transgression of his duty to conduct a fair trial. During jury selection, he ruled again and again that it was all right for jurors to think the defendants were guilty as long as the jurors were willing to say they could change their minds. Gary's rulings consistently favored the prosecution, and he denied defense requests at every turn. When the defendants asked to be tried separately so that the evidence against one of them would not be held against all of them, Judge Gary refused. He gave the prosecution the freedom to present evidence that was only distantly related to the crime while subjecting the evidence of the defense team to stringent standards.

In the American system of justice, each side has a right to question its opponent's witnesses. This process, called "cross-examination," is subject to a special rule: questions asked on cross-examination must be relevant to the topics about which the witness originally testified. But what is "relevant"? That is up to the judge to decide. Gary allowed the prosecution to veer widely from the original questions while strictly imposing the rules on the defense.

A WEAK CASE

After assuring the jury that the case would be based solely upon the facts and that he would not play upon their prejudices, the lead prosecuting attorney, Julius Grinnell, proceeded, in his opening statement, to do everything he could to appeal to the jurors' biases and manipulate their emotions:

> In the light of the fourth of May we now know that the preachings of Anarchy [by] . . . these defendants hourly and daily for years, have been sapping our institutions, and that where they have cried murder, bloodshed, Anarchy and dynamite, they have meant what they said, and proposed to do what they threatened.

The prosecution's two key witnesses told far-fetched stories about overhearing the conspirators discuss their plans right before the bomb went off. First, M. M. Thompson, an employee of the department store Marshall Field & Company, testified that he had followed Spies and Schwab into Cranes Alley, where he overheard them plotting revenge against the police. Thompson swore that he spotted Spies and Schwab passing an object—allegedly, the bomb—to a third man, who put it into his coat pocket. After being shown a photograph of Rudolph Schnaubelt, the Haymarket conspirator who had been released after arrest and was now on the run, Thompson identified him as the third man.

The defense discredited Thompson's testimony by producing witnesses who established that Schwab had been at the Haymarket rally for only a few minutes and that he had left before the meeting began. They also pointed out that Spies and Schwab always spoke to each other in German, a language Thompson didn't know. Further discrediting himself, Thompson admitted on cross-examination that the prosecution had prepped him by showing him a picture of Schnaubelt before the trial.

The prosecution's other star witness, a painter named Harry L. Gilmer, was also hard to believe. Gilmer testified that he had witnessed a clandestine meeting in Cranes Alley between Spies and Fischer and another man—whom he identified in a photograph as Schnaubelt. After watching them confer with one another in hushed tones, Gilmer said he saw Spies light a match and ignite a bomb. But Gilmer's testimony was easily discredited by the defense, who pointed out that he had never before mentioned any of this—neither at the coroner's inquest, nor before the grand jury, nor when, in the presence of reporters, he had told his story to the police. In fact, on another occasion he had identified Fischer as the bomber.

LIBERTY IS NOT ANARCHY.

This illustration, entitled *Liberty, Not Anarchy,* shows the hands of Justice holding, in the left, a sword labeled U.S., and, in the right, a handful of anarchists.

Damaging Gilmer's credibility even further, ten prominent Chicago citizens testified that he was a habitual liar. On cross-examination, Gilmer admitted that he had received money from Detective James Bonfield, the brother of Chief Inspector

Jack Bonfield. In addition, there were many witnesses, including reporters and policemen, who had seen the bomb thrower, and all of them testified that he did not resemble Schnaubelt. Many also testified that the bomb had not been thrown from Cranes Alley, where Gilmer claimed to have seen it thrown, but from Desplaines Street.

After attempting to link the defendants directly to the bomb, the prosecution moved on to the second part of its case. With the cooperation of Gottfried Waller and Bernhard Schrade, two anarchists who had agreed to testify in order to escape being charged with the others, the state's attorney tried to establish that the Haymarket bomb was part of a plan to spark an anarchist uprising—a plan supposedly hatched in a meeting hall the day before the Haymarket incident. Although Waller and Schrade testified that they had heard Engel, Fischer, and Lingg speaking about revolution during that meeting (which was no surprise, considering they were all anarchists), neither went so far as to say that he had heard any of the accused mentioning a bomb or Haymarket Square. The prosecution did manage to prove that Louis Lingg made bombs, but they could not produce any evidence linking Lingg to the particular bomb that had killed Officer Degan.

A third part of the prosecution's case, and the real heart of their courtroom strategy, was simply to present the jury, for days on end, with the most inflammatory speeches and writings of the defendants and of other anarchists not on trial. They displayed an assortment of bombs and bomb parts, none of which had been traced to any of the defendants or to the Haymarket bomb. They laid out the bloodstained uniforms of the policemen for the jury to see.

In their concluding remarks, the prosecution tried to frame the crime as broadly as possible. They maintained that the defendants had been involved in a vast conspiracy to overthrow the social order. Drawing the jury's attention to the idea of a major anarchist plan for revolt, the prosecution urged the jurors to convict the anarchists even if none of the evidence or testimony that had been presented had succeeded in convincing them of the defendants' guilt. One of the prosecutors went so far as to say that not only the eight defendants but three thousand of their fellow anarchists were guilty of Degan's murder.

The defense countered by contending that the defendants were not on trial for being anarchists: they were on trial for one crime—the Haymarket bombing—and one murder—the murder of Officer Degan. Furthermore, they argued, the prosecution had not produced any evidence linking any of the defendants to the Haymarket bomb, nor had they produced any evidence of a specific conspiracy, other than the defendants' general advocacy of anarchism and the use of violence—specifically, dynamite.

The lead prosecuting attorney, Grinnell, rested the prosecution's case by again calling the jury's attention to the dangers of anarchism. He proclaimed that though it was a glorious thing that the United States was a republic, there was "but one step from republicanism to anarchy." Thus, he implied, anarchism posed a greater danger to the United States than it did to other countries and it should be suppressed even more vigorously here than elsewhere. He warned that if the jury freed the anarchists, the anarchists' followers would "flock out again like a lot of rats and vermin."

Judge Gary sealed the fate of the defendants in the instructions he gave to the jury. In a speech that sounded like a closing argument for the prosecution, Gary told the jury that they could find the eight men guilty of murder even if the actual crime had been committed by a person who had not been identified. Echoing the prosecution's message, he implied that anarchism itself was a criminal conspiracy, and because of this, all anarchists could be held equally responsible for a death arising from their beliefs.

THE VERDICT, THE APPEALS, AND THE EXECUTION

On the morning of August 20, 1886, just one day after they began their deliberations, the jurors announced that they had found all eight defendants guilty. They declared that seven of the accused should be sentenced to death (by hanging) and one, Oscar Neebe, to fifteen years' imprisonment. While the evidence presented against the other anarchists does not seem credible today, there had been no evidence at all of a crime committed by Neebe. All that was known was that he was member of anarchist organizations and that a search of his home had turned up two guns, a sword, and a red flag. The presence of these objects in his home was not a crime. Still, he was an anarchist. Thus the jurors did not acquit him, but they gave him a lighter sentence than the other men on trial.

Nina Van Zandt, the Chicago socialite who married August Spies by proxy when he was in prison.

Throughout the United States, the verdict was hailed as a victory of law over anarchy. It was the general consensus of opinion that the Haymarket anarchists (a group of specific men) and anarchism (a political philosophy) were one and the same. With the exception of a few radical papers, newspapers throughout the nation agreed that anarchism had been given a fair trial and that it had been given the only fitting penalty: death.

Lucy Parsons, the wife of Albert, spearheaded the effort to overturn the convictions. She was helped by Nina Van Zandt, a Chicago socialite who had attended the trial out of idle curiosity. Van Zandt was a wealthy heiress, the only child of a Chicago medicine manufacturer. She took up the cause of all the men but was especially drawn to August Spies, with whom she talked for hours through wire mesh when she visited him in prison. Newspapers went wild when it was learned that the glamorous Van Zandt had married Spies by proxy (his brother stood in for him, saying the vows in a ceremony conducted outside the prison).

As tempers around the country cooled, some important national figures began to express misgivings about the trial and question the wisdom of hanging seven anarchist leaders. The novelist William Dean Howells attempted, without success, to convince the editor of *Harper's Magazine* that the trial had been unfair. The banker Lyman J. Gage, who was later made U.S. secretary of the treasury, called a meeting of bankers and businessmen to argue that showing clemency—mercy, forgiveness—to the anarchists would help improve relations between labor and management.

When a trial is thought to have been unfair or impaired by mistakes in law or by faulty evidence, attorneys may ask the judges of a higher court to review the case and reverse the decision, in some cases leading to a new trial. This process is called an *appeal*. Attorneys for both sides of the case then debate the merits of the previous trial before the judges. Attorneys for the Haymarket defendants appealed their case to the Illinois Supreme Court. When the Illinois Supreme Court upheld the original verdict, the attorneys appealed to the U.S. Supreme Court, a very conservative body at the time. Giving in to the fears and prejudices of the day, the U.S. Supreme Court turned down the appeal.

As the date of the executions approached, people friendly to the cause rallied to save the prisoners' lives, beseeching the Illinois governor, Richard J. Oglesby, to commute, or reduce, their sentences. Among those asking the governor to intervene were the conservative labor leader Samuel Gompers and the British writers Oscar Wilde and George Bernard Shaw.

While Oglesby was considering their petitions, news arrived that one of the prisoners, Louis Lingg, had committed suicide by exploding a smuggled stick of dynamite in his mouth. About two hours after Lingg's death, Oglesby announced his decision to lessen the sentences of Fielden and Schwab to life imprisonment. He did not have the legal authority to commute the sentences of the other prisoners because none of them had filed a request for a reprieve.

On November 11, 1887, Albert Parsons, August Spies, George Engel, and Adolph Fischer ascended the scaffold that had been erected in the Cook County prison. Attired in white robes provided by the state for the occasion, the condemned men stood before the row of nooses that awaited them. The bailiff fastened leather straps around their ankles, then proceeded to drape the nooses

An 1887 *Frank Leslie's Weekly* illustration showing the march of the Chicago anarchists to the scaffold before the moment of execution. The frame to the left depicts Albert Parsons singing in his cell.

around their necks. August Spies's rope got caught on his ear, and according to one of the witnesses to the execution, he jerked his head in order to make it fall. Flouting the right of the condemned to say their last words, the bailiff put hoods over their heads before any of them had the chance to speak. The men had to utter their last words from underneath the shrouds that covered their faces. Just before the order came to open the trapdoor beneath them, Spies said from beneath his hood: "The day will come when our silence will be more powerful than the voices you are throttling today." Parsons said: "Will I be allowed to speak, O men of America?" Fielden and Engel shouted, "Hurrah for anarchy!" Then all four men fell at once. Parsons and Engel appeared to die instantly, but it took Spies and Fischer several minutes before they were strangled to death.

To the twenty thousand people who marched behind the funeral procession two days later, the executed anarchists were martyrs. As far as the Chicago Bar

THE MARCH TO THE GRAVE.
THE FUNERAL PROCESSION OF THE CHICAGO ANARCHISTS—PASSING DOWN MILWAUKEE AVENUE.—See page 11.

The funeral of the anarchists was attended by 20,000 people. This illustration appeared in *Frank Leslie's Weekly* at the time.

Association—an organization of the city's lawyers—was concerned, however, justice had prevailed. At a bar association dinner held in his honor six weeks later, Judge Gary was praised for making the legal profession a bulwark—a safeguard—against radicalism and was applauded for decrying the "tyranny" of labor unions.

THE PARDON

In January 1889, the *Chicago Times* reported that Chief Inspector Jack Bonfield and Captain Michael Schaack had been extorting money from saloon keepers, prostitutes, and thieves and that they had been selling merchandise they had confiscated from people they had arrested. Bonfield responded to the article by arresting the newspaper's editors and trying to shut down the *Times*. This, however, was going too far; there was a general public outcry, and the mayor suspended Bonfield and Schaack. After an investigation both of them were fired.

This scandal—disgracing the two policemen who were most closely identified with the Haymarket bombing—gave force to an effort to obtain the release of the three surviving prisoners. An amnesty committee for these prisoners included prominent Chicago citizens who were remorseful about the part they had played in the events leading up to the executions.

By this time, Illinois had a new governor, Joseph F. W. Fifer. A cautious, mediocre politician, Fifer was unwilling to get involved in a controversy and was no help to the committee.

However, the governor elected in 1892, John Peter Atgeld, was a man of a different stamp. A Civil War veteran and former Chicago Superior Court judge, he had risen to state office as a supporter of prison reform. He agreed to listen to the arguments of those who wanted the remaining prisoners pardoned.

Clarence Darrow, who would go on to become the most celebrated trial lawyer of his time, spoke to Governor Atgeld on behalf of the Haymarket defendants. As Darrow recalled later in his autobiography, Atgeld told him to be patient: "If I conclude to pardon these men it will not meet with the approval you expect; let me tell you that from that day I will be a dead man."

On June 26, 1893, after a lengthy review of the trial records, Atgeld issued a full pardon for the surviving prisoners: Fielden, Schwab, and Neebe. As expected, the move was extremely controversial, all the more so because Atgeld justified his decision with a detailed condemnation of the trial. Atgeld wrote that "much of the evidence given at the trial was a pure fabrication." He criticized the judge, the jury, and the people of Illinois. "No greater damage could possibly threaten our institutions than to have the courts of justice run wild or give way to popular clamor."

Newspapers and prominent public officials accused Atgeld of encouraging the overthrow of civilization. The *Chicago Tribune* said that Atgeld, who had been born in Germany, did not have "a drop of true American blood in his veins." The future U.S. president Theodore Roosevelt called him "a friend of the lawless classes." Cartoonists depicted him as a terrorist. Historians have been kinder to the governor, viewing his pardon as an act of moral courage unusual in a professional politician.

THE AFTERMATH

The two decades after the Haymarket trial saw many bitter clashes between labor and management in the United States. This period was also the heyday of international anarchist violence, marked by assassinations and random bombings. In

THE FRIEND OF MAD DOGS.

Governor Altgeld of Illinois in freeing the Anarchists bitterly denounced Judge Gary and the jury that convicted them.

This 1893 cartoon, entitled "The Friend of Mad Dogs," suggests that Governor Atgeld's pardon of the surviving Haymarket defendants, Samuel Fielden, Michael Schwab, and Oscar Neebe, was tantamount to releasing the hounds of socialism, anarchy, and murder. The monument erected in memory of the Chicago police officers who were killed or wounded in the Haymarket Riot is pictured in the background.

1901, Leon Czolgosz, a young man claiming to be an anarchist, assassinated President William McKinley.

These bloody deeds did not bring about the end of private property or cause great numbers of people to rally to the cause of anarchy—indeed, they succeeded in frightening many more people than they attracted. However, it would be glib to say that anarchist violence had no impact on the course of history. The fear of revolution may have made government officials consider the need for reform, in America as well as in Europe. Whatever the reason, the period of American history between the Haymarket bombing and the First World War is often called the "Progressive Era." It was a time during which more and more regulations were imposed on businesses, and business and government alike reluctantly recognized the right of workers to organize. As the efforts of unions and reform-minded politicians brought about tangible changes in the lives of industrial workers, drastic solutions began to have less appeal and the anarchist movement was pushed to the fringes of American society.

Soon enough, though, America would find other devils.

"I think this case will be remembered because it is
the first case of this sort since we stopped trying people
in America for witchcraft, because here we have done our best
to turn back the tide that has sought to force itself
upon this modern world, of testing every fact in science
by a religious dictum. That is all I care to say."
—*Clarence Darrow, at the conclusion of the trial*

Clarence Darrow and William Jennings Bryan in the courtroom in Dayton, Tennessee.

✤ Chapter 3 ✤
The Scopes "Monkey" Trial

In the 1920s, rural Americans saw the work of the devil in the most upsetting trends of modern life—in the defiance of law, in the wild new music called jazz, and especially in the spread of disbelief in the literal truth of the Bible. They passed a law intended to shore up religious faith, and the stage was set for a trial that pitted science against religion.

MODERN TIMES

The 1920s still look modern to us. Anyone comparing photographs taken before World War I to photographs taken afterward can see how suddenly everything seems to change after the war ends. When the twenties arrive, the furniture and the people slim down. The few horses remaining on the city streets look lost amid the automobile traffic. People talk on the telephone, drive cars, listen to radios, and play records on their phonographs. They read tabloid newspapers and film magazines, where they learn from advertisements that they have a disease called halitosis, which can be cured by a product called Listerine. They shop at chain stores, play miniature golf, watch stunt pilots performing in aerial shows, and dance the Charleston. They have a president who tells them, "The business of America is business," and by and large they seem to agree. They're conscious of their modernity and conscious of how much things have changed, though not all of them are happy about it.

Americans of the 1920s also seem contemporary in their tremendous appetite for entertaining news. A man stuck in a mine for weeks, a ballplayer breaking all-time batting records, a young aviator flying solo across the Atlantic—these were

Jazz musicians play and flappers dance the Charleston in the Roaring Twenties. While many Americans celebrated the new freedom of behavior, others decried such scenes as examples of decadence and immorality.

the breaking stories that had the entire nation buying newspapers and tuning in their radios.

In 1925, the story that gripped the country was a trial that dramatized some of the most serious issues of the era, pitting religion against science, the Holy Bible against the theory of evolution, the nineteenth century against the twentieth, rural American against urban America, the great Populist orator William Jennings Bryan against the great agnostic lawyer Clarence Darrow. For eight unbearably hot July days in 1925, the small town of Dayton, Tennessee, would be every newsman's dream. Huge banners proclaiming PREPARE TO MEET THY GOD! SWEETHEARTS, COME TO JESUS! YOU NEED GOD IN YOUR BUSINESS! would be hung from the sides of barns and draped over planks on the courthouse lawn. There would be monkeys dressed in business suits and food vendors selling hot dogs, soda, ice cream, and corn bread. There would be sidewalk preachers and portable toilets. The story that would have Americans glued to their radios that summer began with a scientific theory; a law that was passed, almost by accident, in response to that theory; and a discussion in a local drugstore among an enterprising group of well-meaning friends and neighbors, which culminated in one of the most famous court battles in American history.

THE SCIENTIFIC THEORY

In 1859, the British naturalist Charles Darwin published *On the Origin of Species by Means of Natural Selection,* providing overwhelming evidence for his theory that all species of plants and animals had evolved over the course of many millions of years through a mechanistic process called "natural selection." Not only did this theory of evolution flatly contradict the story of creation as told in the Bible, but it explained the whole concept of creation and creatures without recourse to God, as the outcome of a purely amoral, monumentally indifferent natural process.

For this reason, among others, many people found Darwin's theory to be deeply disturbing.

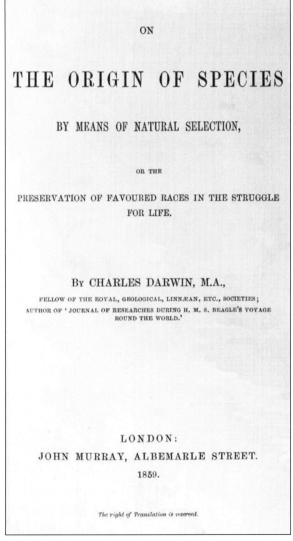

ON

THE ORIGIN OF SPECIES

BY MEANS OF NATURAL SELECTION,

OR THE

PRESERVATION OF FAVOURED RACES IN THE STRUGGLE FOR LIFE.

By CHARLES DARWIN, M.A.,

FELLOW OF THE ROYAL, GEOLOGICAL, LINNÆAN, ETC., SOCIETIES; AUTHOR OF 'JOURNAL OF RESEARCHES DURING H. M. S. BEAGLE'S VOYAGE ROUND THE WORLD.'

LONDON:
JOHN MURRAY, ALBEMARLE STREET.
1859.

The right of Translation is reserved.

Title page of the 1859 edition of Charles Darwin's *On the Origin of Species.*

One religious leader called Darwin "the most dangerous man in England." The geologist Adam Sedgwick said that the theory of evolution was sure to "sink the human race into a lower grade of degradation than any into which it has fallen since its written record tells us of its history." Even those who believed in evolution did not like it. "When its whole significance dawns on you, your heart sinks into a heap of sand within you," commented the British playwright George Bernard Shaw. "If it be no blasphemy, but a truth of science, then the stars of heaven, the showers and dew, the winter and summer, the fire and heat, the mountains and hills, may no longer be called upon to exalt the Lord with us by praise; their work is to modify all things by blindly starving and murdering everything that is not lucky enough to survive in the universal struggle for hogwash."

Scientists were convinced by the theory of evolution, however, because it explained so much and the evidence for it was powerful. Eventually the ordinary newspaper-reading public was convinced as well, partly because evolution is the kind of theory that nonscientists can understand, and that once understood is not easily dismissed. Evolution also gained acceptance because the theory mirrored and seemed to justify the ruthless economic competition of the nineteenth century. Darwin's theory was about struggle. It provided moral ammunition to society's winners by confirming what tough-minded businessmen in England and the United States had always said—government assistance to the weak upsets the order of nature. Only the strong survive, and this, it turns out, is a good thing, because it improves the breed.

By 1920, most religious leaders were able to come to terms with the theory of evolution by deeming the Bible's account of creation to be morally rather than literally true. They were encouraged to reach this conclusion not only by modern biology but also by nineteenth-century linguistic scholarship, which had demonstrated that the Bible was the work of many authors over the course of hundreds of years. To many people this implied that the Bible was a product of the human mind—perhaps divinely inspired, but not infallible.

Religious leaders who reconciled themselves to Darwinism and the new findings of Bible scholarship are sometimes called the "modernists." At the turn of the twentieth century, they represented the mainstream of Protestantism in the United States. Modernists held that scientific and religious truths were different sorts of truth and therefore could not be construed to contradict each other. Children continued to learn the story of Adam and Eve in Sunday school. Meanwhile, without objection from the religious community, Darwinism became a regular part of the curriculum in every public school and every college in the nation.

THE BIRTH OF FUNDAMENTALISM

Not everyone assented to this compromise between science and religion. Modernism might work in the industrial and commercial northeastern states, where people had grown complacent about religion, but in the rural South, religion was still about revival meetings and saving souls. It was about the promise of heaven and the threat of hell, a promise vouched for by the words of the Bible. To question the authority of the Bible was to weaken that promise.

A group of mostly Southern religious leaders decided to erect a wall against religious modernism by publishing a series of pamphlets entitled "The Fundamentals," in which they affirmed their belief in a set of core tenets of Christianity, among them the infallibility of the Bible. First published in 1909, these pamphlets were disseminated free of charge to churches across the nation. The protest against religious modernism was transformed into a formal movement in 1919, when a minister named Dr. William Bell Riley started the World Christian Fundamentals Association. Thus was born Christian Fundamentalism, the fastest-growing branch of Christianity today.

One reason Fundamentalism spread so quickly was that rural Southerners were just as unhappy with other forms of modernism as they were with religious modernism. The economic boom of the 1920s had bypassed many of them. In fact, they felt, with good reason, that this economic boom was being built on their backs. Mechanization, which made farm labor cheaper and more efficient, and the end of the First World War, which in turn led to a decrease in European demand for American farm products (because Europeans were growing their own food again), had led to a sharp, permanent drop in the price of these products: great for city dwellers but a disaster for farmers, many of whom went bankrupt as a result.

It is not surprising, then, that farmers, and the depressed small towns that depended on them, saw the 1920s from a perspective quite different from that of the rest of the country. To them, the immigrants pouring into the seaports were threats to the American way of life and the way things used to be. The flouting of Prohibition in speakeasies, the wild dancing to Negro jazz, the short skirts, the big-city gangsters, the new phenomenon of teenagers necking in cars, the extravagant spending, and the frivolous divorces of Hollywood movie stars were all evidence of the moral decline of the nation. Rural Southerners attributed this decline to a loss of faith in the Bible, and they blamed the loss of faith on Darwin's theory. A prominent Fundamentalist wrote: "All the ills from which America suffers can be traced back to the teaching of evolution!"

This photo of better-than-average housing conditions in the settlement of Dunbar, Louisiana, depicts rural poverty in the South in 1911.

THE BUTLER LAW

In order to fight the insidious influence of evolution, the Fundamentalists lobbied their politicians to pass laws banning the teaching of the theory in public schools. In 1923 alone, anti-evolution bills were introduced in six states. Although a couple of states came very near to making those bills into laws, it wasn't until 1925 that the Fundamentalists finally succeeded in getting a law passed.

The legislator who drafted the Tennessee anti-evolution bill, John Butler, said: "The teaching of this theory of evolution breaks the hearts

John Butler, author of the Butler Law.

of fathers and mothers who give their children the advantages of higher education in which they lose their respect for Christianity. . . . If we are to exist as a nation the principles upon which our Government is founded must not be destroyed, which they surely would be if we became a nation of infidels . . . when we set the Bible aside as being untrue and put evolution in its place."

Butler's law made it a crime "to teach any theory that denies the story of the Divine Creation of man as taught in the Bible and to teach . . . that man has descended from a lower order of animals."

When Butler introduced the law to the state house of representatives, most of the legislators didn't take it very seriously. But, afraid of offending their constituents, they passed it by a vote of 71 to 5. (The speaker of the house was one of the only legislators brave enough to speak out against the bill. Deploring the religious extremism that was behind the Butler law, he called out from the floor: "Save our children for God!") The congressmen assumed that the upper house would defeat the bill anyway. But ironically, when it reached the upper house, the very same line of reasoning prevailed: the politicians there were just as fearful of the political consequences of offending the Fundamentalist voters, and they didn't think their actions would have any real consequence either, since the governor would never sign the bill into law. But much to everyone's surprise, when the bill reached his desk, Governor Peay—who had political considerations of his own— signed the bill. "They've got their nerve to pass the buck to me when they know I want to be United States Senator," he was heard to mutter when he put his signature on the piece of paper.

Peay thought that in any case his act was largely a symbolic one. When he signed the Butler law he made it clear that he had no intention of enforcing it. "Nobody believes it is going to be an active statute," he said.

THE ACLU STEPS IN

At first it seemed as though Governor Peay might be right. After the law's enactment, the state made no attempt to enforce it. There were no plans to revise the state's science courses and its textbooks, all of which contained explanations of the theory of evolution. Even textbooks in the Bible Belt (as journalist H. L. Mencken dubbed the ultrareligious South) carried chapters about Darwin's theory.

At the time of its enactment, most people were not aware that the Butler Act had been passed. The majority of Tennessee papers didn't even bother mentioning it. But when one paper ran a small story with the headline "Tennessee Bans the Teaching of Evolution," it caught the eye of Lucile Milner, the executive secretary of the American Civil Liberties Union (ACLU). Formed in 1920 to defend pacifists who had been arrested for refusing to fight in World War I for reasons of conscience, the ACLU was dedicated to protecting the civil liberties of Americans. Milner could see that the Butler law posed the kind of threat to freedom of speech and religion that the ACLU had been created to combat. When Milner passed the story on to her supervisors, they agreed.

And so the ACLU prepared to set up a "test case."

The initial goal of a test case is to lay the groundwork for arguing the constitutionality of the law in question before a higher court. The ACLU's plan was to work its way through the court system until it reached the Supreme Court. If the Supreme Court found the Butler law unconstitutional, states would be unable to enact similar laws and the Fundamentalist campaign against evolution would be dealt a crushing blow.

The ACLU proceeded to look for a teacher in Tennessee who would be willing to go out of his way to admit that he had taught evolution and then to stand trial for breaking the law. To that purpose, the organization sent a statement to all Tennessee newspapers, offering to pay the legal fees and any costs of a Tennessee teacher willing to be a defendant to test the Butler law. The ACLU ad read, in part: "We are looking for a Tennessee teacher to accept our services in testing this law in the courts. . . . All we need now is a willing client."

THE DRUGSTORE CONVERSATION

When George Rappelyea, a mining engineer in Dayton, Tennessee, noticed the ACLU ad in the *Chattanooga Daily News,* he decided that he wanted to have the test case held in his town. Rappelyea's interest in the case was rooted in the troubling memory he had of a funeral of an eight-year-old boy who had been crushed to death by two coal cars. The Fundamentalist preacher presiding over the funeral had castigated the grieving parents for not having baptized their son. "This here boy . . . is now awrithin' in the flames of hell," he had scolded. Rappelyea, reflecting on the story afterward, said, "Well, a few days later, I heard that this same bunch, the Fundamentalists, had passed that Anti-Evolution Law, and I made up my mind I'd show them up to the world."

Although not all the local businessmen and politicians he invited to attend a meeting at Robinson's Drug Store agreed with Rappelyea's views on evolution, everyone agreed that having the test case in Dayton could be a commercial gold mine for the struggling town. Dayton would be in the news. Visitors would flock to the town, meaning more customers for the local businesses. Possibly even a few of those visitors would decide to make their home in the lovely town, which in recent years had seen its population drop from eight thousand people to three thousand. In anticipation of the event, the town business leaders had a brochure printed that said, "Why Dayton of All Places."

As for who the "willing client" would be, everyone agreed that a young teacher named John Thomas Scopes would be the ideal candidate. John Scopes was single, so he didn't have a family to worry about, and he was popular, so he wouldn't be likely to antagonize the Fundamentalists of Dayton. Eager to get the ball rolling, the men told a boy who was sitting at the fountain sipping a soda to go find Scopes and tell him to come to the drugstore. A little while later, Scopes arrived at Robinson's, drenched with sweat. It was a hot day and he had been playing tennis.

Scopes was uneasy about making himself an object of publicity and about hav-

F. E. Robinson, proprietor of Robinson's Drug Store (fourth from left), helps unload bundles of a sixteen-page booklet, "Why Dayton of All Places?" produced to promote Dayton during the trial.

Robinson's Drug Store on Main Street, Dayton. F. E. Robinson's daughter later described her father as "a promoter. He never missed a chance to promote his business or Dayton." Note the "Where It Started" banner.

ing an arrest record to boot, and at first he declined. But Rappelyea appealed to Scopes's patriotism. Believing it would give him the chance to serve his country, Scopes finally agreed to volunteer.

A shy, quiet man, Scopes comforted himself with the thought that it would probably just be a local matter. After it was all over, he figured he could go ahead with his summer plan, which was to go home to Kentucky and sell cars to raise money for graduate school. Later Scopes would say: "It was just a drugstore discussion that got past control."

BRYAN AND DARROW

And indeed, the trial in Dayton might very well have stayed "a local affair, a case among friends," as Scopes had originally thought it would be, had it not attracted the attention of the great political evangelist William Jennings Bryan. A three-time presidential candidate who had served as the secretary of the state under Woodrow Wilson, Bryan was one of the leaders of the anti-evolution movement. In addition to traveling around the country to speak out against evolution, Bryan had authored many of the anti-evolution bills himself.

On May 13, Bryan announced that he would represent the World Christian Fundamentals Association at the trial, and Fundamentalists across America rejoiced. "We cannot afford to have a system of education that destroys the religious faith of our children," Bryan proclaimed. "There are about five thousand scientists, and probably half of them are atheists, in the United States. Are we going to allow them to run our schools? We are not."

The young William Jennings Bryan, Democratic presidential candidate, 1896.

Bryan decried the changing intellectual tenor of the country, where science was replacing religion as the major intellectual force. "The sin of this generation is mind worship—a worship as destructive as any other form of idolatry," said Bryan. As far as he was concerned, what the country needed was "not more brains but more heart—not more intellect but more conscience." The "Great Commoner," as he was fondly known by hard-pressed farmers of the Populist Party, objected to the theory of evolution on political grounds as well. He had seen Darwinism used to support political and economic conservatism. Darwin had found unbridled competition—the "survival of the fittest"—to be the law of nature. Applied to social and political thought, Darwin's theory could be construed to support the agenda of economic conservatives, who argued against government programs and regulation designed to assist the poor in *their* struggle for survival. From Bryan's perspective, Darwinism meant letting people suffer the consequences of their own supposed incompetence. After reading Darwin's *Descent of Man*, Bryan said, "Such a conception of man's origin could weaken the cause of democracy and strengthen class pride and the power of wealth."

Portrait of Clarence Darrow, taken during the Scopes trial.

The little "local affair" was destined to be less little and local still when Clarence Darrow decided to volunteer his services to the defense. At age sixty-eight, Darrow was the most famous trial lawyer of his time. He was known as a champion of the underdog, a man who took cases that other lawyers considered hopeless. He was also well known for being an opponent of capital punishment (and, in fact, of any punishment—he said the criminals should be "treated" rather than "punished").

Deeply committed to civil liberties, Darrow regarded the anti-evolution campaign as an attack on the Constitution. He was particularly enraged at Bryan for the role he played in mounting this assault. In response to a letter Bryan had addressed to the academic community and the press publicly offering to pay a hundred dollars of his own money to anyone who would sign an affidavit stating that he was personally descended from an ape, Darrow had written a letter of his own. In his letter, published in the *Chicago Tribune,* Darrow submitted a list of fifty-five questions to Bryan, questions concerning familiar biblical anomalies such as how the serpent got around before God punished him by making him crawl on his belly and was Jonah really swallowed by a whale, and if so, how long was it before the whale spewed him out. Bryan had never responded to any of the questions, and Darrow was hoping that the trial would give him the opportunity to pose them to Bryan in person.

At first the ACLU was reluctant to accept Darrow's help. According to Scopes, the ACLU "felt Darrow was a headline chaser, and as a consequence, the real issue would be obscured." The trial "would become a carnival and any possible dignity in the fight for liberties would be lost." But Scopes wanted Darrow to represent him, and the ACLU felt obliged to grant its volunteer defendant his wish.

With Darrow on board, the ACLU had to revise its original goals for the trial, which had been limited to challenging the constitutionality of anti-evolution legislation, pure and simple. Darrow's plan was far more ambitious. He wanted to stage an all-out attack on Fundamentalism. He would invite world-renowned experts in the areas of science and theology to testify about evolution and thereby show that the Fundamentalists were suppressing the teaching of a valid scientific theory. Beyond that, he wanted to expose the dangers inherent in the repressive thinking of the Fundamentalists and their leader, William Jennings Bryan.

Eventually, Darrow prevailed, and with the other members of the defense—which included prominent attorney Dudley Malone, ACLU attorney Arthur Garfield Hays, and Tennessee attorney John Randolph Neal—three general goals were established: First, the defense would educate the judge, jury, and public about evolution. Next, they intended, through the testimony of the scientists and theologians they would assemble, to demonstrate that science and religion were not incompatible. Third, they would address the issue of academic freedom and emphasize that it was crucial for teachers to be allowed to teach unfettered by legislation.

However, whether or not they would be able to follow through on their ambitious strategy would be up to the judge. It was in the prosecution's interest to keep the trial focused on the simpler question of Scopes's guilt and innocence. Did the state have the right to tell teachers, whose salaries they paid, what they had to teach? Yes, indeed they did, and as far as the state was concerned, there were no other issues that needed to be discussed.

THE TOWN PREPARES

Once Bryan and Darrow agreed to participate, it was obvious that the Scopes trial would attract national attention. The citizens of Dayton painted their houses and trimmed their lawns in anticipation of the big event. Businessmen scrambled to prepare Dayton for the onslaught of more than two thousand visitors. They arranged to have the Pullman Company sidetrack cars to serve as sleeping quarters. They secured tents from the War Department; they created a list of citizens who were willing to open up their private homes to visitors. The Aqua Hotel, one of the three hotels in Dayton, raised its rates to eight dollars a night, and the Bailey rooming house set up cots up and down its halls. Privies were installed on the street corners. The courthouse was given a fresh coat of varnish, its benches were painted cherry red, and extra spittoons were ordered. A makeshift pressroom was set up above the hardware store on Main

John Scopes in a photo taken at the time of the trial. Scopes was twenty-three when he agreed to be the ACLU's volunteer defendant in the case that became known as the "trial of the century."

"Mendi" the chimpanzee was brought to the "Monkey Trial" as a publicity stunt.

Street to accommodate the 150 reporters from around the world who would come to cover the "Monkey Trial," as the Scopes trial had already come to be known. Twenty-two Western Union operators were stationed in a room off the town's one grocery store, ready to transmit reporters' stories across the wires to their newspapers, magazines, and radio programs. Hollywood film studios sent motion-picture cameramen to make newsreels of the trial.

Monkey themes started cropping up everywhere. Robinson's Drugstore featured a five-cent "monkey fizz" at the soda fountain. The local butcher shop posted a sign in its window saying WE HANDLE ALL KINDS OF MEAT EXCEPT MONKEY. Merchants displayed cardboard monkeys in store windows; there were stuffed monkeys for sale everywhere. Vendors sold large buttons that said YOUR OLD MAN'S A MONKEY.

The radio station WGN hooked up wires throughout the town and installed dozens of microphones in the courtroom to broadcast the trial, which would be the first in history ever to be aired over the entire country. Outside on the courthouse lawn, loudspeakers were set up to broadcast the proceedings to the visitors, most of whom would not be able to fit into the seven-hundred-seat courtroom. A bandstand was set up as well, and there was even a barbecue pit dug into the lawn.

Fundamentalists poured into the town to witness for themselves the defeat of the atheists at the hands of their champion, William Jennings Bryan. Some families came in covered wagons equipped with beds, some slept outside in tents they'd set up in the parks, and others simply curled up under the trees at night and went to sleep under the stars. The Anti-Evolution League and booksellers set up to hawk their wares, including Fundamentalist favorites such as the best-selling book *Hell and the High Schools* and several books by William Jennings Bryan, as well as Fundamentalist pamphlets and, of course, the Bible. Preachers came to stand on corners and urge people to come to Jesus, and among them were holy men with names like "John the Baptist the Third" and "Deck Carter, Bible Champion of the World." Later, in his autobiography, Darrow would write: "All sorts of weird cults were present in Dayton, all joining forces to put up a strong fight against Satan and his cohorts. It was really another Armageddon."

A crowd of adoring fans were there to greet William Jennings Bryan when he arrived in Dayton. At a banquet given in his honor that night, Bryan asked his audience, "What is the secret of the world's interest in this little case? It is found in the fact that this trial uncovers an attack which for a generation has been made more or less secretly upon revealed religion, that is, the Christian religion. If evolution wins in Dayton, Christianity goes. Not suddenly, of course, but gradually, for the two cannot stand together. They are as antagonistic as light and darkness; as antagonistic as good and evil."

Darrow arrived two days after Bryan. There was no crowd to greet him.

THE TRIAL BEGINS

Judge Raulston, a lay preacher who came to court every day with a Bible tucked under his arm, started the first day of the trial with a prayer, as he would every day for the following eight days. Despite the unbearable heat, the courtroom was jam-packed with people. Trials were a popular form of entertainment for the locals, and the rural courtrooms were built to accommodate large crowds of onlookers. That's why the courtroom in Dayton, a town of under three thousand people, had seven hundred seats, every one of which was taken that Friday, with an additional three hundred people standing at the back of the room.

The temperature in Dayton was ninety degrees in the shade, and, in the words of journalist H. L. Mencken, the courtroom felt like a "blast furnace." The people, equipped with their palm leaf fans, were willing to brave the heat in order to have this chance to bear witness to history in the making. In deference to the heat, the judge relaxed the usual court requirement for formal dress, and the room was a sea of men in white shirts, with their sleeves rolled up, detachable collars off, some replaced by handkerchiefs strategically placed to catch the sweat that dripped incessantly from their necks. (With the exception of a few of the more emancipated women, the audience was male.) In this age before air conditioning, even electric fans were rare, and the judge was the only one who was afforded the luxury of a fan. Later, the sheriff would install ceiling fans to offer relief from the merciless heat.

From left, John Scopes, defense attorney Dr. John R. Neal, and George Rappleyea walk to a court session beneath a banner instructing "Read Your Bible."

Members of the jury, with Sheriff Bluch Harris standing left and Judge John T. Raulston standing right. Front row, from left: W. G. Taylor, Jess Goodrich, Capt. Jack R. Thompson (foreman), William G. Day, R. L. Gentry, and John Wright. Second row, from left: R. L. West, W. D. Smith, James W. Riley, John Dagley, John Bowman. Not pictured: W. F. Roberson.

The first day of the trial was devoted to selecting a jury, which would consist of nine farmers, a farmer-schoolteacher, a shipping clerk, and a fruit grower. All but one belonged to one of the nine evangelical churches in Dayton. Most of the jury had never heard of the theory of evolution.

Dayton was as wholesome and homogeneous as a place could be. There were no Catholics, no Episcopalians, and almost no Jews in this strictly Protestant town, where the major source of entertainment was the church social. People didn't drink or gamble or go to wild parties in Dayton. The women didn't smoke or wear makeup or bob their hair. No woman had ever served on a jury.

It was out of this homogeneous pool of people that the jury was chosen. Yet as similar to one another as they might be, the jurors did not see eye to eye about everything. One member of the grand jury that formally indicted Scopes for his crime said that Scopes should be hanged, while one of his fellow jurors expressed the opinion that perhaps there was something to evolution. "When I was a boy, the Irish potato was called the London Lady and was never larger than a hen's egg. The tomato was a little, ridgy, one-sided thing that no more resembled the Ponderosa of today than a two-cylinder automobile looks like a Rolls-Royce. The cow was a crumply-horned animal that gave about half a gallon of milk a day the three months she wasn't dry—and the milk wasn't as good as that we feed our hogs today. And the razor-back hog looked like a hound dog. Stand beside our current Poland China [hog]—then ask me if I believe in evolution."

DAY TWO: MONDAY, JULY 13, 1925

The jury selection complete, the trial was ready to get under way. Tom Stewart, the head of the prosecution, read the formal indictment against Scopes. Next, it was the defense's turn to enter a plea of guilt or innocence, but instead of entering a plea, John Randolph Neal made a motion for the indictment to be quashed on the grounds that the law Scopes was accused of breaking was unconstitutional. As far as the ACLU was concerned, it wasn't John Scopes who was on trial here, but rather the Butler law. The ACLU would have preferred to dispense with the trial and the irrelevant matter of Scopes's guilt or innocence and go straight to the Tennessee Supreme Court to get the unjust law abolished.

As part of his argument, Neal charged that the Butler law violated the Tennessee state constitution on thirteen different grounds, including disregarding the article that stated, "It shall be the duty of the general assembly to cherish literature and science." In addition, he said, the law violated the prohibitions against state interference with freedom of speech and thought contained in the First Amendment of the United States Constitution, and it also violated the Fourteenth Amendment's prohibition against the state's right to establish a religion.

Next, defense counselor Arthur Garfield Hays spoke. He suggested facetiously that according to the Butler law any theory denying the Bible story that the earth is the center of the universe should be forbidden as well. Underscoring just how unreasonable he found the statute to be, Hays proposed a hypothetical law that would make it illegal to teach that the earth revolved around the sun. Dudley Malone followed by stating that the law should be quashed because it imposed on the people of Tennessee a particular religious opinion from a particular religious book in which not everyone necessarily believed.

The most compelling argument of the day was presented by Clarence Darrow. Stating that he was going to argue the case "as if it were a death struggle between two civilizations," Darrow said:

> Here we find today as brazen and as bold an attempt to destroy learning as was ever made in the Middle Ages. . . .
>
> If today you can take a thing like evolution and make it a crime to teach it in the public schools, tomorrow you can make it a crime to teach it in the private school and next year you can make it a crime to teach it to the hustings or in the church. At the next session you may ban books and the newspapers. Soon you may set Catholic against Protestant and Protestant against Protestant and try to foist your own religion upon the minds of men. If you can do one, you can do the other. Ignorance and fanaticism are ever busy and need feeding. . . . Today it is the public school teachers; tomorrow, the private. The next day the preachers and lecturers, the magazines, the books, the newspapers. After a while, Your Honor, it is the setting of man against man and creed against creed until with flying banners and beating drums we are marching backward to the sixteenth century when bigots lighted fagots to burn the men who dared to bring any intelligence and enlightenment and culture to the human mind.

In response to the defense argument that the trial should be quashed since the idea that Scopes had committed a crime was based on an unconstitutional law, the prosecution maintained that the Butler law was constitutional and that the state had the right to require teachers to teach what they were hired to teach. Announcing that he needed time to consider the two sides' arguments before he reached a decision on the issue, Raulston adjourned the court for the day.

Clarence Darrow addresses the court in Dayton, Tennessee.

DAY THREE: TUESDAY, JULY 14

The fact that Judge Raulston began each session with a Christian prayer had been bothering Darrow since the first day of the trial, but he waited until the court convened the third day to raise the issue to the judge. "This case is a conflict between science and religion," he contended, "and no . . . attempt should be made by means of prayer . . . to influence the deliberation and consideration by the jury of the facts in this case."

Tom Stewart, arguing against Darrow's objection, replied that the case did not have anything to do with ideology; it was about the law, specifically "whether or not a schoolteacher has taught a doctrine prohibited by statute." Then, belying his own words, Stewart proceeded to refer to Darrow as "the agnostic counsel for the Defense." In so doing, Stewart was carrying out the prosecution's plan to besmirch Darrow in the eyes of the jury. One of the prosecutors was quoted in the *Chicago Tribune* as saying: "All we have to do is to get the fact that Mr. Darrow is an atheist and does not believe in the Bible across to the jury, and his case is lost. He will not get to first base here; the jurors will merely yawn. They will listen to no one but Bryan."

After hearing the arguments, Raulston overruled Darrow's objection and the prayer stayed. The judge adjourned court that day at one p.m.

DAY FOUR: WEDNESDAY, JULY 15

On Wednesday morning, Judge Raulston announced his decision against the motion to quash. In a long-winded speech, Raulston argued that the Butler law violated neither religious freedom nor personal liberty and therefore Scopes should be tried.

And so, after a series of false starts, the trial was finally ready to get under way.

After each side outlined its arguments, the prosecution proceeded to present

Judge John T. Raulston reads a ruling to the court.

its case, the high point of which was the testimony of two high school boys who had been prepped by Darrow to testify that Scopes had taught them about evolution.

Once the prosecution had elicited testimony from fourteen-year-old Howard Morgan, establishing that Scopes had taught the class about evolution, it was Darrow's turn to cross-examine the boy. Referring to the boy's acknowledgment of Scopes's evolution lesson, Darrow asked:

"It has not hurt you any, has it?"

"No, sir."

"That is all."

The next prosecution witness was seventeen-year-old Harry Shelton, who, under questioning from the prosecution, testified that Scopes had taught him that all life came from a single cell. In the cross-examination, Darrow asked: "Are you a church member?"

"Yes, sir."

"Do you still belong?"

"Yes, sir."

"You didn't leave church when he told you all forms of life began with a single cell?"

"No, sir."

And so, with all the witnesses examined and cross-examined, the prosecution rested its simple, cut-and-dried case. Now it was the defense's turn.

The entire foundation of the defense's argument lay in the fact that Scopes was accused of committing two separate crimes: one, teaching evolution, and two, contradicting the Bible. The defense never had any intention of challenging that Scopes had committed the first crime. Indeed, their entire strategy rested on the fact that he had taught Darwin's theory of evolution to his students: so as to leave no doubt in the minds of the jury that he had, Darrow declared after the students had testified, "Every single word that was said against this defendant, everything was true."

The only charge that Darrow disputed was the second one, which was, in the words of the Butler law, that Scopes had taught a theory that "denies the story of Divine Creation of man as taught in the Bible." In order to prove that Scopes was not guilty of contradicting the Bible, Darrow sought to prove that the Fundamentalist interpretation of biblical creation—that God had created man in one fell swoop—was by no means an interpretation shared by all Christians. Darrow reasoned that if millions of Christians could reconcile themselves to the idea that man had evolved over a period of hundreds of thousands of years from an infinite variety of organisms, then Scopes had not contradicted the Bible when he taught his class that lesson about evolution.

To that end the defense had assembled a group of expert witnesses, which included fifteen scientists and religious leaders, all of whom had come to Dayton at their own expense to testify on behalf of religious and academic freedom.

With the help of the expert witnesses, Darrow had intended to give the

Some of the scientists brought to testify for the defense.

country a gigantic lesson in evolution. To begin that lesson, he called to the stand Maynard A. Metcalf, a professor of zoology at Johns Hopkins University. As anticipated, the prosecution voiced its objection to Metcalf's testimony, pointing out that such testimony was irrelevant to the case, since Scopes's guilt or innocence had nothing to do with the truth or untruth of evolution. But Judge Raulston said that he would allow Metcalf to testify, for now. It would serve as a kind of sample on which the judge would base his final decision as to the admissibility of such testimony. The audience sat in rapt attention as they heard Metcalf talk about evolution, how it was about "the change of one organism from one character into a different character." At the end of the day, when student Harry Shelton's mother was asked what she thought about the teaching of evolution after hearing what Metcalf had to say about it, she said, "As far as I'm concerned, they can teach my boy evolution every day of the year. I can see no harm in it whatsoever. Why, when they called Bud [*sic*] to testify against Mr. Scopes, he had forgotten most of his lessons. He had to get the book out and study it up."

DAY FIVE: THURSDAY, JULY 16

The next day was devoted to the debate over whether scientific testimony would be admitted into evidence. Darrow began with a prepared statement:

> We expect to show . . . first, what evolution is, and, secondly, that any interpretation of the Bible that intelligent men could possibly make is not in conflict with any story of creation, while the Bible, in many ways, is in conflict with every known science, and there isn't a human being on earth believes it literally.

After lunch, William Jennings Bryan got up to speak on behalf of the prosecution. This was the moment that everyone had been looking forward to. Clutching a textbook containing a chapter about evolution in one hand and a palm fan in the other, Bryan proclaimed that he wouldn't permit any more of this "pseudoscientific" material to be interjected into the trial.

William Jennings Bryan addresses the court.

"The people of this state knew what they were doing when they passed the law," he said, "and they knew the dangers of the doctrine so that they did not want it taught to their children. And, my friends, it isn't—Your Honor, it isn't proper to bring experts in here to try to defeat the purpose of the people of this state by trying to show that this thing that they denounce and outlaw is a beautiful thing that everybody ought to believe in." Bryan proceeded to ridicule Metcalf for having the audacity to say that human beings shared the same biological heritage as mere animals:

> They were teaching your children that man was a mammal and so indistinguishable among other mammals that they leave him there with three thousand four hundred and ninety-nine other mammals, including elephants. . . .

New York Times headline, July 17, 1925: "Bryan Defends Tennessee and Its Law; Calls Evolution Attack on Church; Spirited Debate on Expert Evidence."

The Bible is the word of God; the Bible is the only expression of man's hope of salvation. . . . The Bible is not going to be driven out of this court by experts who come hundreds of miles to testify that they can reconcile evolution with its ancestor in the jungle, with man made by God in His image, man put here for purposes as part of the divine plan.

People in the audience called out "Amen!" and "Yes! Yes!" When Bryan finished speaking, they piled out of their seats, and with tears in their eyes, they thanked him for speaking for them.

After a short recess, defense attorney Dudley Malone rose to address the court. Throughout the trial, while all the other men removed their jackets and opened their shirt collars in search of relief from the sweltering heat, Malone had maintained the appearance of absolute cool. His apparent imperviousness to the heat had become something of a curiosity to everyone. Now Malone took off his coat and folded it neatly on the table. "Mr. Bryan, Your Honor, is not the only one who believes; he is not the only one who believes in God; he is not the only one who believes in the Bible."

The audience, still bathing in the afterglow of Bryan's stirring speech, slowly began to realize that here, too, was someone who had something important to say. "Keep your Bible," Malone exhorted the audience.

Keep it as your consolation, keep it as your guide, but keep it where it belongs, in the world of your own conscience, in the world of your individual judgment . . . and do not try to tell an intelligent world and the intelligence of this country that these books written by men who knew none of the accepted fundamental facts of science, can be put into a course of science, because what are they doing here? . . . We have just had a war with twenty million dead. Civilization is not so proud of the work of the adults. Civilization need not be so proud of what the grown-ups have done. For God's sake, let the children have their minds kept open—close no doors to their knowledge; shut no doors from them. Make the distinction between theology and science. Let them have both.

The courtroom exploded with an enthusiasm that surpassed that which it had expressed for Bryan. One of the policemen, caught up in the excitement of the crowd he was there to control, pounded a table with his nightstick so hard that he split the top of the table.

Amid the uproar, Bryan sat, looking dejected and alone. In his memoir, John Scopes wrote about watching Bryan at that moment, "reading the tragedy on his beaten face."

Day Six: Friday, July 17

That morning, Raulston announced his decision to exclude expert testimony. Although this came as a terrible blow to the defense team, they felt that all would not be lost if they would at least make the experts' testimony available for future reference when the case went to a higher court. With this in mind, Darrow asked the judge for permission to spend the rest of the day entering the experts' affidavits into the court record, and when Raulston expressed his reluctance to allot so much time to the task, Darrow erupted in anger:

"I do not understand why every request of the state and every suggestion of the prosecution should meet with an endless amount of time, and a bare suggestion of anything that is perfectly competent on our part should be immediately overruled."

"I hope you do not mean to reflect upon the court?"

"Well, Your Honor has the right to hope."

The judge responded by threatening to charge Darrow with contempt of court.

With Raulston's ruling, the defense had no case to present. There would be no more lessons about evolution, and no more arguments about whether or not such lessons were relevant to the trial of John Scopes. From all appearances it seemed that the most exciting part of the trial was over, and just as suddenly as the hordes of people had descended on Dayton, so suddenly did they all begin to leave: the newspapermen packed up their cameras and typewriters and notepads, the radio engineers packed up their wires and microphones, the visitors bundled their chairs and their families back into their wagons, and the exodus from Dayton began. Anything to follow would be anticlimactic. There was no doubt in anyone's mind that Scopes, absent a defense, would be judged guilty as charged, so there didn't seem to be much point in enduring the unbearable heat any longer.

DAY SEVEN: MONDAY, JULY 20

The day that everyone expected to be nothing more than a routine wrap-up of business would turn out to be the most exciting of the trial. As expected, Raulston

Clarence Darrow, right, questions William Jennings Bryan, left, on the courthouse lawn during the seventh day of the trial.

charged Darrow with contempt for his insolence the previous day, Darrow apologized, and it seemed that all that remained was to send the jury out to make its foregone decision.

The court recessed for lunch, and when it reconvened, Raulston announced that he was moving the trial outside. According to rumor, there were signs that the ceiling might crack, but according to some historians, Raulston just wanted an excuse to get out of the stifling heat of the courtroom.

After people had taken their places on the lawn and Darrow had registered his protest against a huge sign outside the courthouse that said READ YOUR BIBLE (suggesting that it be accompanied by a sign that said READ YOUR EVOLUTION), everyone got ready for a relatively uneventful wind-up of the trial. But then, in a move that stunned everyone, the defense asked to call William Jennings Bryan to the stand.

By putting the world-renowned Fundamentalist on the witness stand, Darrow was going to find out once and for all just how infallible the Bible was. Against the protest of the other members of the prosecution team, Bryan took the stand. He welcomed this opportunity to defend the Bible against the self-proclaimed agnostic's assault. He lounged in his chair under the pine and oak trees on the platform that had served as a podium for the Fundamentalist preachers who had come in droves to Dayton that July, as Darrow, acting very friendly, began his questioning.

After Bryan had confirmed that yes, he believed that everything in the Bible was literally true, Darrow proceeded to quiz him on just how literal he believed the Bible to be. Darrow began slowly, but soon he was firing questions at Bryan one after the other. Did he believe the Bible story about the whale swallowing Jonah? Did he believe that Joshua had made the sun stand still, and if so, did he ever wonder what happened to the earth as a consequence? Did he realize that it would have been converted into "a molten mass of matter"? He asked Bryan about the Flood and whether he could give a date when exactly it had occurred.

Darrow continued along in this vein until Bryan was so flustered that his hands trembled. Then the great lawyer set his final trap:

"Do you think the earth was made in six days?" he asked.

"Not six days of twenty-four hours," Bryan, near witless with frustration and rage, answered.

In his memoir, John Scopes wrote: "These were astonishing answers. When Bryan admitted the earth had not been made in six days of twenty-four hours, the Fundamentalists gasped." Bryan had just denied the literal interpretation of the Creation.

Bryan, furious with Darrow, blurted out that Darrow only wanted to "cast ridicule on everyone who believed in the Bible."

To which Darrow responded: "We have the purpose of preventing bigots and ignoramuses from controlling the education of the United States and you know it, and that is all."

Darrow picked up the Bible: "'And the Lord God said unto the serpent, Because thou hast done this, thou art cursed above all cattle, and above every beast of the field; upon thy belly shalt thou go and dust shalt thou eat all the days of thy life.' Do you think that is why the serpent is compelled to crawl upon its belly?" he asked.

"I believe that," Bryan responded.

Darrow wanted to know how the serpent went about before that time. "Did he walk on his tail?" he asked. The audience burst into laughter, and Bryan scowled at them.

In a rage, Bryan lashed out at Darrow. Shaking his fist at him, he said, "I am simply trying to protect the word of God against the greatest atheist or agnostic in the United States," he said.

With that, the judge adjourned the day's session.

DAY EIGHT: TUESDAY, JULY 21

When court opened the next day, Judge Raulston officially expunged Bryan's testimony from the record. In his opinion, it did not shed any light on the issue of whether or not Scopes had taught that man descended from a lower order of animals, which, the judge asserted, was the subject of the trial—not what role God had to play in man's development. With no more witnesses, Darrow rested his case. Now it was up to the jury to decide.

Judge Raulston called in the jury, who had been absent from the proceedings for almost the entire trial. The members of the jury, who had expected to have front-row seats at the trial that held the world in its thrall, had spent most of their time out on the courthouse lawn, where Judge Raulston had banished them so that they would not be privy to discussions he deemed to be irrelevant to matters of John Scopes's guilt or innocence. In an ironic twist, the judge had apparently forgotten about the loudspeakers that had been set up outside the courthouse. The jury had heard the entire proceedings.

Nine minutes later, the jury returned with its verdict of guilty. With that, Judge Raulston fined Scopes one hundred dollars.

William Jennings Bryan stayed in Dayton, polishing up a speech reaffirming his religious and political beliefs, a speech he hoped would redeem his reputation in the eyes of the world. But he died in his sleep five days after the trial ended. He was sixty-five years old.

THE AFTERMATH

The ACLU never got the chance to bring the Butler law to the higher courts. The Tennessee Supreme Court reversed the decision of the jury in the Scopes trial on a technicality: by levying the fine himself, Judge Raulston had violated the state constitution, which required that all fines greater than fifty dollars be levied by a jury. When a decision is reversed, the case is usually returned to the lower courts to be retried, but the Tennessee Supreme Court urged the state to drop the matter, stating: "We see nothing to be gained by prolonging the life of this bizarre case."

There was no clear winner in the Scopes trial. It could be said that in certain respects it was a victory for the civil libertarian cause of fighting for freedom of

Pallbearers load the casket containing the body of William Jennings Bryan onto the train that carried it to Washington, DC, for funeral services and burial at Arlington National Cemetery.

speech and thought. For one thing, the trial dramatized the issue of academic freedom. Also, because of the bizarre spectacle of the Scopes trial, states were wary of ever actually enforcing their anti-evolution legislation. And with the humiliation of William Jennings Bryan and his subsequent death, Fundamentalists had lost their leader.

In other respects, though, the Scopes trial was more of a victory for the Fundamentalists. Emboldened by Scopes's guilty verdict, they went on to wage a campaign to get anti-evolution laws passed throughout the country. William Bell Riley, leader of the World Christian Fundamentals Association, declared: "Within twelve months, every state in the Union will be thoroughly organized."

Although Riley's prediction did not come true—only two states passed anti-evolution legislation, Mississippi in 1926 and Arkansas in 1928—the ACLU was unable to find another teacher willing to volunteer for a test case. Eventually the organization stopped pursuing the matter, declaring that the law was essentially meaningless since it was never enforced.

But even though the laws against teaching Darwin's theory of evolution were not enforced, the theory was eliminated from science curriculums across the country. Most teachers were afraid to teach it, lest they lose their jobs. And so, despite their lack of success in the legislative arena, Fundamentalists succeeded in virtually halting the teaching of evolution in public schools across the nation for the next thirty-odd years. Some publishers—including the publisher of the book Scopes had used—deleted all mention of evolution from new editions of their biology texts. In Texas, Governor Miriam Ferguson ordered that all references to evolution be literally cut out of textbooks used in the schools. Ferguson declared: "I'm a Christian mother who believes Jesus Christ died to save humanity, and I am not going to let that kind of rot go into Texas textbooks." In Mississippi, one of the states that had passed an anti-evolution law, a high school superintendent held a public bonfire of the pages about evolution that had been torn from the textbooks used in his school.

It wasn't until 1957, in reaction to the news that the Soviets had beat the Americans in putting the first artificial satellite into space, that the unofficial ban on the teaching of evolution in the public schools was lifted. The idea that the Soviet Union could surpass the United States panicked Americans, who then focused their attention on improving science curriculums, which had been seriously damaged by the wholesale exclusion of this basic biological fact. One result of this new initiative was the development of a series of textbooks that featured evolution as the backbone of biology.

The ACLU did not have the opportunity to bring the issue of teaching evolution to the Supreme Court until 1968, in a case challenging the 1928 Arkansas anti-evolution law. In *Epperson v. Arkansas,* the Supreme Court declared the law to be unconstitutional on the grounds that it violated the separation of church and state required by the First Amendment of the U.S. Constitution. The civil libertarians prevailed again in 1987 when the ACLU challenged the constitutionality of a Louisiana law that required the teaching of "creation science," a theory promoted by the Fundamentalists.

Fundamentalism remains a powerful and fast-growing religious force in the United States today. Fundamentalists are allied with the modern evangelical Protestants, who share their views regarding the literal truth of the Bible. Conservative Christians have never let go of their hostility for Darwinism or their frustration over the fact that their children may learn on weekdays a doctrine that undermines the beliefs their pastors instill in them on Sundays. They still consider Darwin's theory to be the work of the devil, and they have continued to launch a series of increasingly sophisticated assaults on the teaching of evolution in public schools.

Instead of attempting to ban Darwinism from the schools altogether, the strategy of conservative Christians is to change the curriculum to remind students that evolution is merely a theory, and to teach it along with alternative hypotheses such as "creation science" and "intelligent design." This approach attempts to sidestep questions about the separation of church and state, since the other theories need not mention God or the Bible. Civil libertarians insist that creationism and intelligent design are at best very bad science and that teaching them side by side with evolution is like teaching children that the earth might be flat and the stars might be holes in the sky. Neither the civil libertarians nor the Fundamentalists are likely to compromise anytime soon.

"Mr. Hiss represents
the concealed enemy
against which we are
all fighting."
—*Whittaker Chambers*

"Getting the facts about Whittaker Chambers,
if that is his name, will not be easy. . . .
His operations have been furtive
and concealed. Why?
What does he have to hide?"
—*Alger Hiss*

Alger Hiss testifying at his trial.

✤ *Chapter 4* ✤

The Trials of Alger Hiss

Seldom has the world seemed so starkly divided between light and dark as it did in the late 1940s, when politicians began speaking of a struggle between Communism and the free world. Only a few years earlier, history's most destructive conflict, World War II, had ended with the use of the atomic bomb, raising the stakes of war forever. Looking at Soviet Russia, many Americans saw a totalitarian country bent on taking over the world. Looking at American Communists, they saw the enemy within.

"WE ARE CAUGHT IN A TRAGEDY OF HISTORY"

In the late 1940s, Americans were crossing into a kind of promised land. They had slogged their way through the Great Depression and the Second World War, they had worked and suffered, and they were about to be rewarded. The most prosperous era in United States history was under way. More Americans than ever before were marrying and having children. Outside the cities, bulldozers were leveling hills to ready them for mass-produced houses with lawns and swing sets, preparing for the suburban life that would seem typically American in the years to come. Television, which would play a central role in that life, was just catching on. In 1948, only around 100,000 people had their own sets. All across the country, shoppers stood outside appliance-store windows, mesmerized by the flickering black-and-white images on the rows of new TVs. It was a period of rapid transition, bringing new hopes and new anxieties. People looked forward to having a television, and they worried about inflation, and the atomic bomb, and Communism. Especially, in 1948, they worried about Communism.

On August 25, 1948, television cameras were brought into a large, crowded room in the Capitol Building in Washington, DC, for a hearing of the House Un-American Activities Committee (HUAC). A conservative group created by Congress in the late 1930s, HUAC had assumed the role of national watchdog against Communism, the influence of which HUAC seemed to see everywhere. The congressmen of HUAC were not publicity shy, and their committee had just stumbled onto the biggest case of its career.

The tiny new TV audience and the much larger radio and newspaper audiences were about to witness an amazing drama. In HUAC hearings earlier that month, Whittaker Chambers, a senior editor at *Time* magazine, had leveled a shocking accusation against Alger Hiss, the president of the Carnegie Endowment for World Peace. Chambers accused Hiss of being a secret member of the Communist Party. Chambers said that he and Hiss had worked together in the Communist underground during the 1930s. Chambers added that he and his wife had developed close, personal friendships with Hiss and his wife, Priscilla, who was also a Communist.

If proven, these charges would end Alger Hiss's career and cause political damage to everyone who had been connected with him, including some of the most important people in the U.S. government. If Chambers was telling the truth, then Alger Hiss had been a party member while he worked at the U.S. State Department, the government agency responsible for American foreign policy. He might even have been a Communist when he was assistant to the assistant secretary of state, a job that had given him direct access to the president, perhaps influencing his views on the Soviet Union.

Hiss and Chambers had each testified separately before the committee earlier that month. Alger Hiss had denied Chambers's accusations. Today, for the first time, they were testifying at the same hearing in public. It was a kind of showdown.

A photograph taken that day shows the accuser, Whittaker Chambers, leaning forward on his elbows. He is a heavyset man, and his pale suit is stretched taut across his round shoulders. His fingers are splayed over the triangular base of

Whittaker Chambers (right), *Time* magazine editor, takes the stand before the House Un-American Activities Committee on August 25, 1948, reiterating his testimony that Alger Hiss was a secret Communist, as Alger Hiss (circled) looks on.

a shiny, fist-size microphone—one of several that rise up from a tangle of black wires before him. The microphones make the picture typical of a certain kind of news photo of that period. Microphones took up a lot of space in the 1940s—at press conferences and hearings, they were the sign that something important was being said, something every citizen should know.

One of the HUAC congressmen asked Whittaker Chambers how he felt about Alger Hiss. Chambers replied slowly in measured phrases. "The story has spread that in testifying against Mr. Hiss, I am working out some old grudge, or motives of revenge or hatred. I do not hate Mr. Hiss. We were close friends, but we are caught in a tragedy of history. Mr. Hiss represents the concealed enemy against which we are all fighting, and I am fighting. I have testified against him with remorse and pity, but in the moment of history in which this Nation now stands, so help me God, I couldn't do otherwise."

INTERNATIONAL COMMUNISM AND AMERICAN COMMUNISM

Most of the people in that room knew what Whittaker Chambers meant when he said that he and Alger Hiss were "caught in a tragedy of history." For Chambers, and for millions of other Americans, the conflict between these two men was the central drama of their time. It was as if an international struggle between good and evil had come down to Whittaker Chambers and Alger Hiss. In fact, Chambers and many of his fellow anti-Communists wouldn't have said "as if." They saw Chambers's testimony as a turning point in world history. America had been sleeping for too long. If Whittaker Chambers could not make himself believed, then America might not wake up in time.

To understand how so many people could have read so much into a war of words between two men, one needs to know what was going on in the world in the late 1940s. While many Americans were enjoying prosperity, some of them were also very frightened. Looking abroad, they saw a determined enemy getting stronger every day.

The Second World War had taken the lives of fifty million people and had left all the great international powers crippled, except for two: the Soviet Union and the United States.

These two countries stood for different ways life and forms of government. The United States was a democracy. Its economic system was capitalism—as many Americans preferred to say then, the "free enterprise system"—a system in which industry is under private ownership. The United States was a rich country, but far from perfect. Many of its citizens suffered from racial discrimination and were denied their constitutional rights, and capitalism had led to big inequalities between the rich and poor.

The Soviet Union was also a democracy—that is, officially. The economic system of the Soviet Union was Communism, which had been invented as an answer to the problems of capitalism. Under Communism, the state owned all large enterprises—the factories, the farms, the stores. In theory, this meant that the people of the Soviet Union owned all this property. For this reason, many people around the world, including some in the United States, believed the Soviet Union was a wonderful place. But Soviet democracy was a sham. Soon after the 1917 revolution that brought the Communists to power, the Soviet Union had become a one-party dictatorship in which dissent was not tolerated. Over the years, millions of Soviet citizens suspected of being enemies of the state had been worked to death in slave labor camps. Millions of other Soviet citizens were informers for the secret police, and people could not speak freely for fear their friends and neighbors might report them to the authorities.

Now the Soviets and the Americans, each side with its sharply different set of ideas, faced each other across the smoking rubble of the world's bombed-out cities. Despite its enormous size and power, the Soviet Union always seemed to feel threatened, and was always trying expand its sphere of influence. If they could get away with it—so Whittaker Chambers and other anti-Communists like him insisted—the Soviets would dominate the world, and therefore a fight between the two great powers was inevitable. But, the anti-Communists maintained, so far only the Soviets seemed to realize it, and because they had figured it out before the Americans, they had struck the first blows and were already winning.

The war's end had left the Soviet Union's Red Army in occupation of Eastern Europe, which the Soviets had taken over as they pushed out the Germans. The Soviets had promised their allies, England and the United States, that they would let the countries of Eastern Europe decide their own destinies. But instead, the Soviet Union proceeded to turn them all into little replicas of itself, each a so-called people's republic with a hammer-and-sickle flag, a state-controlled press, a secret police, and a Communist dictator. In 1948, Soviet-controlled North Korea, too, went Communist. And at the very moment that the Hiss case began in the United States, civil wars were going on in China and Greece that would determine whether these countries would suffer the same fate. The Communists had chosen the color red as their symbol; if they had their way, the whole world would soon be red.

How had the Communists achieved this stunningly swift success? The Red

Army's occupation of Eastern Europe at the end of the Second World War was only half of the answer. The other half was that the Soviets had been helped by homegrown Communist parties within each of the countries they had overtaken. Communism as an idea and a political program had been around for a hundred years. All over the world there were Communist parties. All over the world there were Communists—marching with signs, handing out leaflets, organizing strikes, and plotting the revolution that would bring about a world without war, poverty, or class differences. Ever since 1917, when Russia (later called the Soviet Union) became the world's first Communist country, Communists everywhere had looked to the Soviet Union for guidance, sure that it represented the best hope for humankind. In each country that had come under Soviet influence, a local Communist Party had opened the door for the Russians and local Communists led the new Communist government.

America, too, had a Communist Party. True, it was very small. There were never more than eighty-four thousand official members, a fraction of one percent of the American population. But the congressmen of HUAC pointed out that the Communists who had taken over Russia in 1917 had been a small group, too. And, they claimed, official party membership was only the tip of a vast iceberg of secret Communist sympathizers who merely pre-

In the late 1940s and early 1950s the menace of homegrown Communists became the subject of numerous books and movies.

tended to be loyal Americans. These people occupied key positions and influenced U.S. politics—they would be ready to sabotage U.S. industry whenever the order came down from the world Communist headquarters in Moscow. Some people actually believed that American Communists could bring about a Communist revolution in the United States. Many more were convinced that American Communists, acting on secret orders from the Russians, could weaken the United States in its international conflict with the Soviet Union.

So now there was a great debate going on in the United States. What should be done about America's own Communist Party? Did Americans have the right to be Communists? Was Communism a legitimate political viewpoint that Americans had a right to hold even though it was unpopular? Which was more important, homeland security or civil liberties—the political freedoms guaranteed by our Constitution, the freedoms that made America *different* from the Soviet Union? Should Americans be permitted to be Communists just as they were permitted to be Democrats and Republicans? Or was American Communism a conspiracy? Were American Communist Party members simply traitors, working for the victory of the enemy in the undeclared cold war between the United States and the Soviet Union?

Mainstream party politics added to the confusion. Conservative politicians like those who controlled the House Un-American Activities Committee tended to lump liberals and leftists of every type together with Communists. To them, the socially progressive programs that President Franklin Roosevelt had created in the 1930s smacked of Communism. Defenders of these programs—programs such as social security and unemployment insurance—were suspicious of HUAC's activities. As liberals saw it, the conservatives who controlled HUAC were abusing their investigative powers. Conservatives claimed they were saving the nation from an internal Communist conspiracy. Liberals believed that what Conservatives really wanted was to discredit the Truman administration (in office since 1945) and the Roosevelt administration that had come before it.

Under the circumstances, Americans found it difficult to treat Whittaker Chambers's accusation of Alger Hiss objectively. From the outset and for decades

This cartoon by John Herbert, which was published in the *Saturday Evening Post,* depicts labor and the New Deal as being a mask for Communism.

to come, party politics and the cold war would color nearly everyone's perception of the case.

There was one thing everyone agreed on: either Hiss or Chambers was lying. Chambers said the two of them had been Communists together for years. Hiss said he hardly knew Chambers. As the controversy grew, people began to wonder about these two men, both outwardly respectable, who told such contradictory stories. Who were they, and what had brought them to face each other, amid flashbulbs, microphones, and TV cameras, as opponents in the most sensational case of the 1940s?

THE LONG JOURNEY OF WHITTAKER CHAMBERS

In the 1920s, Whittaker Chambers was a young Columbia University student with a troubled home life. He joined the American Communist Party soon after the suicide of his brother. According to his 1952 autobiography, *Witness,* Chambers became a Communist because Communism offered an answer to the two great problems of his time: the problem of wars, and the problem of recurring economic crises. He became a Communist because he believed it was the right thing to do. Chambers said this was what motivated most Communists. They were idealists, and this, he said, was what made them so dangerous.

Chambers worked briefly for the Communist newspaper the *Daily Worker* and then for the *New Masses,* a Communist literary monthly magazine. Eventually he was recruited by Soviet military intelligence. They told him to pretend to quit the party so that he could join the Communist underground and work secretly to promote the party's goals. Following orders from the Soviet Union, Chambers stopped going to party meetings, stopped working for Communist publications, and cut off all public ties with members of the Communist Party. For several years Chambers worked for Soviet spy networks in New York and Washington. He said that it was in his capacity as a secret Soviet operative that he made the acquaintance of Alger Hiss.

In 1938 Chambers quit the Communist Party for real. According to his testimony before HUAC, he quit because he was disenchanted with Communism. The Soviet dictator, Joseph Stalin, had by then killed millions of his own people. He had starved them to death with artificially created food shortages. He had systematically worked them to death in slave labor camps. He had murdered every major leader of the revolution that had originally brought the Communists to power in Russia. Stalin had turned the Soviet Union into a police state, where people were encouraged to inform on each other and were afraid to speak their minds even when they were in the company of friends. Stalin's government also had a habit of inviting American Communists suspected of disloyalty to pay a visit to Russia. Rumor had it that sometimes these American visitors were killed or sent to the labor camps. Chambers had recently received one of these alarming invitations, so the instinct for self-preservation may have played a role in his decision to leave the party.

For a while Chambers went into hiding, afraid that the Soviets might have him killed to prevent him from telling what he knew about the party underground. According to his autobiography, this was just what he intended to do from the moment he decided to leave the party. In 1939, some friends in the anti-Communist movement arranged for him to meet privately with the assistant secretary of state, Adolf A. Berle, Jr. Identifying himself only by his underground name, "Karl," Chambers told Berle about Communist spy networks in the government. He named several people as secret Communist Party members—among them Alger Hiss, who at that time was working for Berle.

During the 1940s, every now and then FBI agents would interview Chambers about the government officials he had named as Communists. Chambers, who had become a deeply religious Quaker, made a new life for himself as a writer and editor for *Time* magazine. At *Time,* Chambers developed a reputation as a zealous anti-Communist and a fierce critic of the Soviet Union.

Chambers's hostility toward the Soviets was unusual in the early 1940s. After 1941, when Adolf Hitler invaded the Soviet Union and declared war on the United States, Russia and the United States were allies, fighting the same enemy. The bloodiest battles of the Second World War took place in the Soviet Union, which suffered more than twenty-five million war deaths, compared with two million British and four hundred thousand Americans. It was in America's interests to support the Soviet war effort, supplying the Soviet Union with food, fuel, and weapons. It was important, therefore, that the American public view the Soviets favorably. The United States government saw no point in playing up the threat of Communism. Most American newspapers, magazines, movies, and radio programs helped to promote a pro-Soviet attitude, and most Americans shared it. The villains on the world stage in the early 1940s were Nazi Germany, Fascist Italy, and the Japanese Empire. The Russians were on our side.

American public opinion changed gradually with the end of the war, as those Eastern European countries—Poland, Hungary, Czechoslovakia, Romania, Bulgaria, and Yugoslavia—all became Communist countries dominated by the Soviet Union. The map of the world was turning red. Americans began to wonder why, and for many the answer was clear: U.S. foreign policy was being undermined by secret Communists in American government. In this political climate, the House Un-American Activities Committee stepped up its investigation of

American Communists. HUAC served Whittaker Chambers with a legal order to testify before the committee on August 3, 1948.

Chambers began testifying before HUAC in a small room, with only committee members and their assistants present. Untidy-looking and talking in a gloomy monotone, he made a poor first impression on the committee members. However, as they listened to him read his prepared statements in his funereal drone, the explosive nature of what he was saying began to dawn on them. Interrupting Chambers, one of the

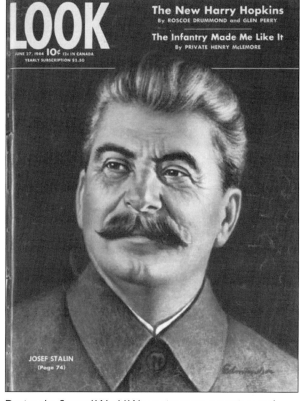

During the Second World War, mainstream magazines and newspapers depicted Joseph Stalin as a good, kind man and the Soviet Union as a nation of heroes.

committee members exclaimed, "Hell, why is this in executive session? This should be in the open!" To Chambers's silent horror—for he had hoped to get this over with quickly and quietly—the other committee members agreed to move the hearing to a room big enough for a large audience.

And so, in the enormous Ways and Means Committee Room, this time with newspaper reporters present, Chambers repeated his statement. He had worked with Alger Hiss, among others, in the Communist Party underground until the late 1930s. He had left the party because he no longer believed in what it was doing. In his last meeting with Alger Hiss, he had begged Hiss to leave the party, too. It was an emotional meeting for both of them, Chambers said; Hiss had wept. "But," said Chambers, "he absolutely refused to break." Chambers added, "I was very fond of Mr. Hiss."

"I AM NOT AND NEVER HAVE BEEN A MEMBER OF THE COMMUNIST PARTY"

In the 1940s, an attack on someone's good name was called a "smear." This expression seemed especially apt with respect to Whittaker Chambers's accusation of Alger Hiss, because the reputation of Alger Hiss was a beautiful object polished to a high sheen. Alger Hiss was the scion of an old Baltimore family. His people were not the sort who became Communists. Though highly respectable, the Hiss family was not wealthy, and Alger Hiss had risen in his profession through hard work, high intelligence, and personal charm. Everyone who knew him was impressed by his honesty and integrity. His career was not a shadowy one—there were no detours on the path of his life. He had been a brilliant student at Johns Hopkins University and Harvard Law School, and his first job following graduation had been as a law clerk for the legendary Supreme Court

During the Great Depression of the 1930s people stood in breadlines to get food that was distributed by charities.

justice Oliver Wendell Holmes. After a brief stint in corporate law, he returned to Washington in the 1930s to participate in the exciting early days of the New Deal, when the Roosevelt administration was seeking fresh young minds to cope with the national crisis of the Great Depression.

Hiss had performed so well at each task given him that he was rewarded with even greater responsibility. He assisted at the 1944 Yalta Conference, where the leaders of Great Britain, the United States, and the Soviet Union made plans for the postwar world. At Yalta he had sat just behind the U.S. secretary of state Edward R. Stettinius and President Franklin Roosevelt. He was chosen to preside at the San Francisco Conference where the United Nations had been organized and had come very close to being the first secretary-general of the United Nations. He was now president of the Carnegie Endowment for World Peace, a post for which he had been recommended by John Foster Dulles, a future secretary of state and a dedicated foe of Communism. Alger Hiss had won the trust of the most influential and admired men and women in America, including two Supreme Court justices and Eleanor Roosevelt, the widow of President Franklin Roosevelt.

Even some HUAC members had trouble believing that this man was a Communist. In the American mind a Communist was an unnatural person, and Americans expected Communists to have certain identifying marks. Ideally, a Communist woman was brisk and masculine. A Communist man was sly and effeminate, or hysterically angry. He should have, if possible, a foreign accent. If he was a native-born American he should still be physically unprepossessing. A Communist was a loser. Only that could explain why he had become a Communist, a choice many Americans found hard to understand in any other terms. In a movie, Whittaker Chambers, with his untidiness, his pasty complexion, and his whiny voice, would have made an excellent Communist. Alger Hiss, with his crisp intelligence, his forthright directness of address, and his amazing list of accomplishments, did not fit the part at all.

On August 5, 1948, when Hiss first replied to Chambers's accusations, he made a very good impression on everyone watching. His voice was firm and clear. He began by reading a statement he had prepared for the committee: "I am not

Alger Hiss sits behind Secretary of State Edward Stettinius Jr. and President Franklin Roosevelt at the February 1945 Yalta Conference, where Hiss was an important American staff assistant. Others around the table include Winston Churchill and Joseph Stalin.

and never have been a member of the Communist Party. I do not and never have adhered to the tenets of the Communist Party." He then went on to deny that he had ever even "laid eyes on" Whittaker Chambers. After he was shown a photograph of Chambers, Hiss said he did not recognize the man. But, Hiss added, he could not swear, just on the basis of a photograph, that they had never met. He asked to see Chambers in person as soon as possible.

Alger Hiss was so effective that day that the committee's members regretted their hasty decision to make Chambers and then Hiss testify in public. They had put their reputations and the reputation of HUAC on the line; now they looked reckless and foolish. One of the Republican members of the committee said, "We've been had! We're ruined." A reporter for the *Washington Post* told the congressmen, "This case is going to kill the Committee unless you can prove Chambers' story." Another HUAC congressman said, "Let's wash our hands of the whole mess," and suggested that the committee send the testimony of both witnesses to the U.S. attorney general, Tom Clark, and let Clark figure out which of the two men was lying. Tom Clark was no friend of HUAC, so this would have been a desperate move.

CONGRESSMAN NIXON'S PLAN

At this point, Richard Nixon, an ambitious young congressman from California who would later become president, came up with another plan. Nixon pointed out that Hiss had not only said that he was not a Communist, but also said he had never even *met* Whittaker Chambers. Surely the committee could settle at least that question before it gave up on the investigation. Since Nixon was willing to stick his neck out, the committee decided to make him head of a subcommittee to look into the question of whether and how well Whittaker Chambers knew Alger Hiss.

That decision would make Richard Nixon famous. In secret sessions in New York City and Washington, Nixon's subcommittee interviewed Whittaker Chambers, Alger Hiss, and several other people who might be able to verify or discredit Chambers's testimony. To prove that he had known Alger and Priscilla Hiss intimately in the 1930s, Chambers gave the subcommittee mundane details about the daily life of Alger and Priscilla at that time—information about their cars, houses, and hobbies. The subcommittee then questioned Hiss, alone, on the same details.

Hiss answered carefully and reluctantly. Even so, some of his memories supported Chambers's story. After taking another look at photographs of Whittaker Chambers, Hiss volunteered a piece of new information. He said that his wife had, for a short time, been acquainted with a down-on-his-luck freelance writer named George Crosley. Crosley had borrowed money from them, said Hiss. It was possible that Crosley and Chambers (who admitted to having used fake names) were one and the same person.

On August 17, 1948, at the Commodore Hotel in New York, Nixon and his colleagues interviewed Alger Hiss again. Then, in a carefully planned surprise intended to rattle Alger Hiss, a door opened and in stepped Whittaker Chambers, who had been waiting in another room. Nixon said, "Mr. Hiss, the man standing here is Mr. Whittaker Chambers. I ask you now if you have ever known that man before."

Alger Hiss later wrote that Chambers at that moment was "perspiring and very pale" and that he "would not meet [his] eye, but stared fixedly before him or up at the ceiling."

Chambers also wrote about this meeting. He described his feelings: "I was swept by a sense of pity for all trapped men of which the pathos of this man was the center. For the man I saw before me was a trapped man."

Hiss, who said he remembered George Crosley as having bad teeth, asked Chambers to open his mouth and then asked him to speak. Chambers read a few sentences from an article in *Newsweek*. At last Hiss said that Chambers was probably the man he and his wife had known as George Crosley.

After the meeting in the Commodore Hotel, Alger Hiss struck back at Chambers and the committee. In a letter released to the newspapers, Hiss said accusations were being leveled against him with a political purpose, "to discredit recent great achievements of this country in which I was privileged to participate." As for Chambers, Hiss questioned his character: "Is he a man of consistent reliability, truthfulness and honor: clearly not. . . . Indeed, is he a man of sanity? Getting the facts about Whittaker Chambers, if that is his name, will not be easy. . . . My own counsel have made inquiries in the past few days and have learned that his career is not, like those of normal men, an open book. His operations have been furtive and concealed. Why? What does he have to hide?"

Finally, on August 25, 1948, in the first congressional hearing ever shown on television, the two men confronted each other in public. The session lasted for nine and a half hours. Hiss was questioned first. Using information gathered from many sources, the HUAC questioners were able to raise strong doubts about Hiss's previous testimony. Hiss was far less persuasive than he had been in his earlier public appearance before the committee. During most of his time at the microphone, he was on the defensive. His answers were nimble but unconvincing, hedged with phrases such as "to the best of my recollection." Still insisting that Whittaker Chambers was practically a stranger to him—just a deadbeat who had borrowed money from him ten years ago—he challenged Chambers to repeat his accusations outside the hearing, where he would not be immune to being sued for libel—communicating false information about a person, damaging his reputation.

Whittaker Chambers spoke to the committee after Hiss. He called Hiss's testimony "80 percent at least fabrication."

THE SLANDER SUIT

Two days later, on August 27, Whittaker Chambers repeated his accusations against Alger Hiss on the radio program *Meet the Press.* By doing this, he was answering Alger Hiss's challenge to accuse him in a forum where, under the law, Chambers could be sued. On September 27, Alger Hiss filed a civil action suit for slander against Whittaker Chambers for his statements on *Meet the Press.*

Slander, like *libel,* means making false and damaging statements about a person (slander refers to spoken statements, libel to written statements). A suit for slander is a civil action—an action between two private individuals or groups—as opposed to a criminal trial, which is between the government and an individual or group. In his slander suit, Alger Hiss demanded that Whittaker Chambers pay him fifty thousand dollars for damaging his reputation. Chambers told reporters, "I welcome Mr. Hiss's daring suit. I do not minimize the audacity or the ferocity of the forces which work through him. But I do not believe that Mr. Hiss or anybody else can use the means of justice to defeat the ends of justice."

The lawyers for Alger Hiss and Whittaker Chambers prepared to do battle in the slander trial. Alger Hiss's attorneys hired private investigators to dig up information that would cast Chambers in a bad light. A psychiatrist consulted by Alger Hiss's lawyers obliged them by saying that Chambers "had a homosexual attraction toward Alger Hiss which caused him to identify himself with Hiss to

A man reads the newspaper, seemingly unaware that Whittaker Chambers is sitting next to him.

desire to possess him and to destroy him." The psychiatrist also said that Chambers, who had earned money as a translator, was trying to act out the plot of a novel he had once translated from German. In the novel, *Class Reunion,* two former classmates meet in a courtroom. One of the classmates has become a judge; the other is the accused.

In fact, during the 1930s, before his religious conversion, Whittaker Chambers had had sexual relations with men, as well as with women other than his wife. Chambers told the FBI about these episodes because he expected them to come up in the trial. They would be considered relevant to his credibility as a witness, since many psychiatrists in the 1940s saw homosexuality as a symptom of mental illness.

Under the rules concerning discovery (the gathering of evidence before a trial), each side must show the other side, in advance, what evidence it plans to introduce, and anyone who has knowledge about a case must cooperate with the lawyers on both sides. So, in preparation for the slander trial, Chambers's lawyers interviewed Alger and Priscilla Hiss. Hiss's lawyers, in turn, interviewed Whittaker Chambers and his wife, Esther. Alger Hiss's lawyers were pleased with the results of their first interview with Chambers. Chambers admitted to a complicated life full of devious behavior. As he himself had confessed, for years he had been a spy practicing constant deception. It would be easy to portray him as a liar.

However, Whittaker Chambers had an unpleasant surprise for the Hiss defense team. He had been hiding evidence damaging to Alger Hiss, and he was about to reveal it.

NEW EVIDENCE AND A NEW ACCUSATION

On November 14, 1948, Chambers went to the Brooklyn home of his nephew. There, from behind a dumbwaiter, he retrieved a stained manila envelope containing five rolls of microfilm, sixty-five retyped pages of State Department papers, and four notes in the handwriting of Alger Hiss. He handed the papers and Alger Hiss's handwritten notes over to Hiss's attorney, withholding the microfilm for future use. The papers that Chambers handed over at this time came to be known as the Baltimore Documents, because Chambers gave them to Hiss's lawyers in Baltimore. They contained information concerning Japanese activities in China, a matter of great interest to the Russians in the 1930s. "I thought I had destroyed them," said Chambers almost apologetically. They were evidence that Hiss had been not just a Communist Party member but a spy. Chambers said that in the late 1930s, when he was acting as a go-between for Soviet military intelligence, Alger Hiss had passed these documents to him. Hiss had brought them home from his State Department office in his briefcase. Priscilla Hiss had typed copies of them, and then Hiss had taken the originals back to the office so that they would not be missed.

As Arthur Conan Doyle, the author of the Sherlock Holmes detective stories, had noticed long ago (in the story "A Case of Identity"), manual typewriters are unique on close examination. With the help of tiny irregularities in the type, experts can match typing to a certain machine in much the same way criminologists are able to match fingerprints to a particular set of fingers. Together with Chambers's testimony, proof that these papers had been typed on Alger Hiss's typewriter would amount to proof that Alger Hiss had been a Communist spy.

The discovery of the Baltimore Documents changed the nature of the Hiss case in two ways. First, the papers provided tangible evidence to support Whittaker Chambers's claim that he and Hiss had worked together in the Communist underground, thereby protecting Chambers from the charge of slander. Second, they were evidence of espionage. To be a Communist was unpopular in the America of the late 1940s, but it was not a crime. Espionage was a

Reporters and photographers mob Whittaker Chambers outside the courtroom after he finished testifying to the grand jury.

crime. In all his previous testimony, Chambers had denied that Hiss was a spy. He later said that he had been trying to protect Hiss, whom he still regarded as a good—though misguided—man. But now, pushed into a corner by Hiss's attorneys, Chambers said that he had no choice but to reveal the true nature of his relationship to Alger Hiss.

Early the next month, Whittaker Chambers gave HUAC investigators more evidence against Hiss: two strips of developed microfilm and three rolls of undeveloped microfilm. The five rolls of film contained additional secret documents, allegedly taken from State Department offices by Alger Hiss. Some of them were telegrams that had been originally transmitted in code. By comparing the translations in their possession with intercepted messages that were still in code, the Soviets could have broken the U.S. diplomatic code, making it much easier for them to spy on the United States. Since Chambers had hidden the rolls of film containing these documents temporarily in a pumpkin on his farm, the newspapers dubbed this new batch of evidence the Pumpkin Papers.

As a result of the Baltimore Documents and the Pumpkin Papers, everyone involved in the slander suit—Hiss, Chambers, their attorneys, and the judge assigned to the case—agreed to put a temporary halt to it. They did so because it was possible that, based on the new evidence, the Justice Department would charge somebody with a crime, and that case, whatever it was, would probably have a great bearing on the charge of slander; it might prove that Chambers had been telling the truth.

But *who* was going to be charged with a crime—Hiss, Chambers, or both of them? For a while it looked as though Whittaker Chambers might be charged with perjury (lying under oath), since he had told two contradictory stories. He had first denied that Hiss had been a spy; then he had changed his story and produced evidence that Hiss had indeed been a spy. But the Justice Department finally decided not to prosecute Whittaker Chambers. Technically he had committed perjury, but he had been providing useful information to the government since 1938, and punishing him would discourage other ex-Communists from coming forward. Even worse, it would have branded Chambers, the star witness against Alger Hiss, a liar. The case against Hiss was more important. In the end there were two trials, both entitled *U.S. v. Alger Hiss.*

THE FIRST TRIAL

Alger Hiss was charged with perjury rather than espionage. If a certain amount of time elapses between the commission of a crime and the discovery of a suspect, the suspect cannot be prosecuted for it. For each crime a different amount of time is specified—that period is the crime's "statute of limitations." Espionage has a five-year statue of limitations, which had already expired by the time Chambers admitted that he—in collusion with Alger Hiss—had committed the crime back in the 1930s. So an espionage charge was out. But Hiss had told several lies under oath, saying he had never been a Communist, he did not divulge State Department secrets, and he did not know Whittaker Chambers. The prosecution would have to get Hiss on perjury charges alone.

Much of the testimony in the case concerned Hiss's typewriter. According to FBI experts, documents typed by Priscilla Hiss in the early 1930s, such as a school application for her son, matched the typing on the Baltimore Documents. In the months leading up to the trial, the FBI had sent hundreds of agents out searching for the typewriter that the Hiss family had owned in the 1930s. The typewriter was finally located, not by the FBI, but by investigators for the Hiss defense team. According to both FBI experts and experts hired by the defense, it was the typewriter that had been used to retype the State Department documents. Alger and Priscilla Hiss said that to the best of their recollection, they had given the typewriter to the family of their maid, Claudia Catlett, some time in 1937—

United States Supreme Court justice Felix Frankfurter testified in defense of Alger Hiss.

that is, before the dates on the Baltimore papers. Members of Claudia Catlett's family backed up the defense's timeline. The prosecutors sought to prove that Claudia Catlett and her family were covering up a lie out of loyalty to the Hiss family. Neither side was able to establish the exact date on which the typewriter had changed hands. But if the typewriter had not been in the possession of Alger and Priscilla Hiss in 1938, how did secret State Department documents come to be typed on it? Hiss's lawyers did not have a convincing answer to this question.

As it had planned to do in the slander trial that never took place, the Hiss defense focused on character—the character of Alger Hiss and the character of his accuser, Whittaker Chambers. No defendant in criminal history ever had a finer group of character witnesses than Alger Hiss. Two United States Supreme Court justices, a United States admiral, a former solicitor general, a former presidential candidate, and a future presidential candidate all testified to Hiss's honesty and loyalty. Meanwhile, the defense's psychiatric witnesses presented elaborate theories about the workings of Whittaker Chambers's supposedly unbalanced mind. In his summation, one of Alger Hiss's lawyers called Chambers "a moral leper."

The first trial ended in a hung jury: the twelve jurors could not agree on a verdict. Eight believed that Alger Hiss had been proven guilty. Four did not. The law required a unanimous decision, so Alger Hiss would have to be tried again.

THE SECOND TRIAL

Defenders of Alger Hiss often point out that his second trial took place in a different world than the first one, even though it began only four months later. Between the first and the second trials, the Soviet Union exploded an atomic bomb, ending the U.S. monopoly on nuclear weapons. The two greatest nightmares for America in the late 1940s had become one nightmare: the Communists had the Bomb. Communism was more frightening than ever.

As in the first trial, however, the prosecution did not base its case on the threat of Communism but on many small details that pointed toward Hiss's guilt. Their case had to do with documents that established links between Hiss and Chambers, with inconsistencies in the testimony of defense witnesses, and above all with the typewriter that had been used to type State Department documents in 1938. The defense in the second trial made even greater efforts to convince the jury that Chambers was a psychopath. The psychiatrist who thought that Chambers was acting out the plot of the novel *Class Reunion* was called to the witness stand to explain his theory.

The jury in Alger Hiss's second trial took twenty-four hours to find him guilty of perjury. The judge gave Alger Hiss permission to make a brief statement before a sentence was passed. "I would like to thank Your Honor for this opportunity to deny the charges that have been made against me," said Hiss, asserting that he had been framed. "I only want to add that I am confident that in the future the full facts of how Whittaker Chambers was able to carry out forgery by typewriter will be disclosed. Thank you, sir."

THE LONG AFTERMATH OF THE HISS CASE

By the time the verdict came, the Alger Hiss case stood for more than the question of whether one man had committed espionage in the 1930s and lied about it ten years later. It had become one of the most politically charged cases in American history. For liberals, who had supported Hiss until his conviction, the verdict was a reason to search their souls—how could they have been so profoundly deceived? For conservatives, it was the chance of a lifetime.

Ever since the election of President Franklin Roosevelt in 1932, liberal Democrats had dominated American politics. They had made sweeping changes, greatly enlarging the role of government in American life. The 1948 presidential election, won by Harry Truman, had given them the White House for another four years, guaranteeing an even twenty years of Democratic rule. For conservative Republicans, Hiss's conviction in 1949 was a godsend. They could now portray all those years of liberal Democratic control as years of treason. Just think of it—the man who had sat behind Franklin Roosevelt at the Yalta Conference had been a spy. His real loyalty had been to Stalin, the Soviet dictator on the other side of that big round table. FDR had been a sick man at Yalta—in photographs taken at the time he looks bleached and haggard—and he died soon afterward. In the imagination of angry Republicans, if not in fact, Alger Hiss had whispered into the ear of a dying FDR to tell him to trust Stalin.

Republicans believed that Eastern Europe had been given away to the Communists at Yalta. This charge was repeated again and again in the early 1950s, usually coupled with the name Alger Hiss.

On February 9, 1950, Republican senator Joseph McCarthy of Wisconsin made a Lincoln Day speech to the Ohio County Women's Republican Club in Wheeling, West Virginia. McCarthy waved a piece of paper, saying that he had "here in [his] hand" a list of 205 Communists who were currently employed by the State Department.

As time would prove, McCarthy was lying, and he did not even bother to be particularly careful about his lies—the number of Communists on his list had a way of changing every time he mentioned it. McCarthy referred to Alger Hiss several times in his Lincoln Day speech and he mentioned Hiss frequently in later speeches. Despite his inconsistencies and carelessness, McCarthy gained immense national attention in the years that followed. He became the head of a Senate subcommittee to investigate Communists in the government and took

Senator Joseph McCarthy, right, with his aide, Roy Cohn.

over the leadership of the anti-Communist movement that dominated American politics for the first half of the 1950s.

For years McCarthy conducted baseless investigations that spread fear and conformity throughout the country. The hunt for Communists, ex-Communists,

This cartoon, created by Marcus Edwin, shows Senator Joseph McCarthy, who has painted himself into a corner using the "red paint" of his accusations (of Communists in government). The cartoon was created in March 1950, two months after McCarthy began his hearings. Although it suggests that McCarthy's smear campaign would soon fail, he was not discredited until 1954.

and people who had been too friendly with Communists moved beyond the government to Hollywood, to labor unions, to journalism, and to the universities and high schools. Former Communists who refused to "prove their loyalty" by identifying other Communists ("naming names") lost their jobs and had their reputations ruined. Lists of people who had belonged to organizations linked to the Communist Party were published, and those on these lists were blacklisted, prevented from getting jobs in the professions they had been trained for. Here and there a liberal objected: Wasn't informing one of the uglier aspects of life in Communist countries? Was the United States, too, going to become a nation of informers? Was American democracy really too weak to tolerate dissent? But liberals were on the defensive during the 1950s, afraid of being called soft on Communism. To prove their loyalty and toughness, many of them would name any Communists they happened to know while at the same time denouncing McCarthy and HUAC for asking them if they knew any.

The successful prosecution of Alger Hiss in 1949 went a long way toward making the reckless accusations by Joseph McCarthy credible in the early 1950s. The conviction also helped to make Richard Nixon famous as an anti-Communist crusader, leading Dwight D. Eisenhower to choose him as his running mate in the 1952 presidential election. In a speech on television, Nixon pointed out that the Democratic candidate, Adlai Stevenson, had submitted a statement for the defense during the Hiss trial. Nixon said he didn't doubt Stevenson's "loyalty," but the question was "one as to his judgment." Eisenhower was elected, and Nixon became vice president.

Eventually, liberals recovered from the 1950s anti-Communist hysteria, regaining control of Congress and the White House, and convincing American voters that they were not "soft on Communism." They were able to do so because Senator Joseph McCarthy, during his four-year red-hunting rampage, was unable to find another Alger Hiss. It also helped that liberal Democrats such as presidents John F. Kennedy and Lyndon Johnson assumed the leadership of the cold war—they supported an arms race against the Russians, and the two countries manufactured enough nuclear bombs to destroy all life on Earth. In the

1960s, still earning their anti-Communist credentials, liberal Democrats led the country into a disastrous war in Vietnam in order to prevent that country from being taken over by Communists.

WAS ALGER HISS FRAMED?

Alger Hiss spent three and a half years at the federal penitentiary in Lewisburg, Pennsylvania, before being released on parole. He served his sentence with dignity, winning the respect of other prisoners. After his release from prison, Hiss published a book, *In the Court of Public Opinion,* in which he again said that he had been framed. In the later 1950s and early 1960s, Alger Hiss worked hard in low-paying jobs unrelated to politics. Always comporting himself admirably, he continued to insist that he had never been either a Communist or a spy.

Over the years, several books have supported the idea that Hiss was framed. Each book tends to have a different theory as to how and why this might have been done. In some theories Richard Nixon or HUAC helped Whittaker Chambers to fake evidence against Hiss. In others the FBI was the chief culprit.

CONSPIRACY THEORIES

These conspiracy theories got a boost in 1968, when Richard Nixon was elected president of the United States. To a new generation of liberals and radicals, the evil of Richard Nixon was a basic fact of life. It wasn't hard to believe that the man Democrats called "Tricky Dick" might have broken the law back in 1948, helping to frame an innocent man, and there was a certain fitness to the idea that Nixon's whole career rested on a fraud.

In 1973, an investigation into the burglary of the Democratic National Committee headquarters at the Watergate Hotel uncovered President Nixon's complicity in many abuses of governmental power. Nixon was forced to resign from office, and his disgrace gave new life to the Hiss defense. During the Watergate scandal the country learned that for years all conversations in the Oval

Richard Nixon leaving the White House after his resignation on August 9, 1974. Nixon became the first U.S. president to resign when the investigation of the Watergate break-in brought to light his administration's many abuses of executive power. Because of Nixon's role in the Hiss investigation in the 1940s, his resignation gave hope to those who believed that Hiss had been wrongly convicted.

Office had been taped. Transcriptions of these tapes revealed Nixon talking obsessively about the Hiss case. In one conversation, Nixon complained of how little help he had gotten from the FBI back then. The White House's transcription reads, "Then we got the evidence, we got the typewriter, we got the Pumpkin Papers. The FBI did not cooperate." Alger Hiss promptly pointed to this tape—and, specifically, to the phrase "we got the typewriter"—as evidence for his "forgery by typewriter" theory. On May 3, 1974, the *New York Times* published an interview with Alger Hiss, headlined ALGER HISS SEES 4 WORDS IN NIXON TRANSCRIPT AS CHANCE FOR EXONERATION. However, a later transcription of the same tape, which had been recorded with better equipment, has Nixon saying "Piper" (the name of one of Hiss's attorneys) rather than "typewriter." In any case, both the phrases "we got the typewriter" and "the FBI did not cooperate" are vague, and apart from Nixon's famous willingness to bend the law, there is no reason to think they refer to anything illegal. The typewriter was indeed missing at one point during the case, and it was found. And though Alger Hiss's defenders would like to interpret "the FBI did not cooperate" to mean "the FBI didn't help us with our plan to frame Alger Hiss," it seems more plausible to think that it means "the FBI did not help us with the prosecution of Alger Hiss."

In the 1970s, more than thirty thousand pages of FBI documents related to the Hiss case were released. Alger Hiss officially requested that the 1949 verdict be overturned on the grounds that he had not received a fair trial. His request was denied. A longtime Hiss loyalist, John Lowenthal, defended Hiss in a documentary film, *The Trials of Alger Hiss.*

In 1991, the Soviet Union broke apart. Most of its former citizens turned out to be sick of Communism, and many of its secrets were disclosed. The following year the Hiss case made headlines again. General Dimitri A. Volkogonov, a Russian military historian with access to the Soviet archives, released a letter saying, "Not a single document . . . substantiates the allegation that Mr. A. Hiss collaborated with the intelligence services of the Soviet Union."

Finally, it seemed, Alger Hiss was vindicated. Proof at last. He *was* innocent.

This conclusion turned out to be premature, however. Volkogonov had spent only two days looking through the relevant files. In December 1992, Volkogonov told the *New York Times,* "I was not properly understood. The Ministry of Defense also has an intelligence service, which is totally different, and many documents have been destroyed. I only looked through what the KGB had. All I said was that I saw no evidence." Volkogonov blamed Alger Hiss and John Lowenthal for the statement that he now regretted making. "His attorney, Lowenthal, pushed me hard to say things of which I was not fully convinced."

Other evidence released in the 1990s has tended to support Whittaker Chambers's charges. In secret files that formerly belonged to Russia's Foreign Intelligence Service, a series of 1936 memos and dispatches refers to Alger Hiss by name as an enthusiastic Communist agent who wanted to help in the recruiting of other agents among his left-leaning acquaintances in Washington. In addition, declassified CIA intercepts of Soviet cables—telegraph communications between Soviet intelligence agents and their superiors—refer to Hiss by his code name, "Lawyer."

There is no such thing as absolute proof. Documents can be forged; the experts who attest to their authenticity might be mistaken or lying. To believe in Hiss's innocence, one must believe in an elaborate and improbable conspiracy. Still, there are intelligent people who remain unconvinced of Alger Hiss's guilt.

Though not everyone agrees about his guilt even today, in 1949 Alger Hiss received a fair trial based on evidence rather than fear. In this respect, the American legal system performed better than the rest of the country did. In the court where he was tried for perjury, Hiss was just a man who had lied under oath. Outside the courtroom, in the eyes of people who had lost their sense of perspective, he became something far more frightening and unreal. He became an agent of the devil as the myth of his awesome power to change the course of world history grew, and his name was used to smear everyone who had innocently befriended him and honestly defended him.

"After all we are in AMERICA,
and everything is possible."
—Zacarias Moussaoui

The Empire State Building and the World Trade Center in New York City on September 11, 2001.

✦ Chapter 5 ✦
The Trials of Zacarias Moussaoui

On September 11, 2001, nineteen fanatics—certain they were doing God's work—conducted the most devastating surprise attack on American soil since Pearl Harbor. The American people then became mentally prepared to let their government bend whatever rules had to be bent in order to win the War on Terror. A new devil had been found, and the American legal system was in jeopardy.

FLIGHT SCHOOL

In Eagan, Minnesota, not far from Minneapolis, the Pan-Am International Flight Academy trains airline pilots with the help of flight simulators—machines that never leave the ground but give a convincing foretaste of flying. From the outside, a flight simulator looks like a white metal shack surrounded by fences and cables. Inside, each one is the exact duplicate of an airliner cockpit, with its complex displays of lights and switches. As a student works the controls, the machine tilts and pitches, and screens present the visual illusion of takeoff and landing and movement over land and water. A flight simulator cannot give the feeling of acceleration, but otherwise it realistically represents the way a particular aircraft would behave in flight.

Most Eagan students are experienced pilots, licensed to fly smaller planes and sent by their respective airlines to study at the flight school. Occasionally, a wealthy man takes the course just to see what it would be like to fly a commercial jet. In 2001, the school had a new student who appeared to be of the rich-man variety. His name was Zacarias Moussaoui, and he had applied to the school by e-mail. His message, in broken English, had been addressed to the flight academy's sales director, Matthew Tierney.

> Hello, Mrs. Matt, I am Mrs. Zacarias. Basically I need to know if you can help to achieve my "goal" my dream. I would like to fly in a "professional" like manners one of the big airliners. The level I would like to achieve is to be able to takeoff and land, to handle communication with ATC. . . . In a sense, to be able to pilot one of these Big Bird, even if I am not a real professional pilot.

Moussaoui was trying to use the slang of the trade: "ATC" is air traffic control, and a "big bird" is a jumbo jet. He explained that although his previous experience was limited to training in a single-engine Cessna at another flight academy in Oklahoma, he wanted to fly a simulated journey from New York to London in a 747-400, a Boeing aircraft that seats more than five hundred passengers. Knowing his prior flight experience was inadequate, Moussaoui wrote, "But I am sure that you can do something. After all we are in AMERICA, and everything is possible." The school accepted him. He arrived in Eagan in early August of 2001.

From the beginning, this new student struck the staff of the flight academy as odd. Moussaoui paid most of the $8,300 fee in hundred-dollar bills. He didn't have a pilot's license. He described himself as an international business consultant, but that was hard

Zacarias Moussaoui's mug shot.

A flight simulator like the one Zacarias Moussaoui used for training at the Pan-Am International Flight Academy in Eagan, Minnesota.

to believe: what business consultant doesn't use a credit card and dresses, as Moussaoui did, in a T-shirt, jeans, baseball cap, and tennis shoes? Moussaoui didn't look like the kind of man who would be able to throw around so much money for a course of instruction that he said was merely "an ego trip." When his instructor asked if he was a Muslim, Moussaoui looked startled and replied sharply, "I am nothing!" At one point, he asked if it was possible for a pilot to shut off the supply of oxygen to the passengers.

THE SEARCH WARRANT

Moussaoui's instructor summed him up as "just a weird duck" and wondered if teaching him to fly was a good idea. The flight academy's manager of pilot training was also alarmed; he called up Pan-Am headquarters in Florida to voice his

U.S. Department of Justice

Federal Bureau of Investigation

In Reply, Please Refer to
File No.

Minneapolis, Minnesota
August 31, 2001

MOUSSAOUI, ZACARIAS;
IT - OTHER

■ This entire communication is classified SECRET.

■ Nature of Investigation: International Terrorism (199M-MP-60130).

■ Full Field Investigation Initiated: 08/15/2001 (NONUSPER).

■ Purpose of this document: To advise the Federal Aviation Administration (FAA) of a potential threat to the security of commercial aircraft.

■ Investigative Background

■ This investigation was initiated after Minneapolis received information from Timothy Nelson, employed by Pan Am International Flight Academy, 2600 Lone Oak Point, Eagan, Minnesota, telephone (651) 208-1253, that he and co-workers were training a student they considered suspicious.

■ Pan Am International Flight Academy's Eagan Facility is a fully accredited flight training center which uses flight simulators to train airline pilots from all over the world. Training conducted there consists exclusively of initial training for persons far advanced in becoming airline pilots, or update/refresher courses given to active airline pilots. In both cases the typical student holds a Federal Aviation Administration (FAA) Airline Transport Pilot (ATP) rating or foreign equivalent and has at least two thousand flight hours.

■ Nelson indicated that Zacarias Moussaoui, who met neither of the above criteria, had been in contact with his company's headquarters in Miami, Florida and had paid $8,000-$9,000 dollars in cash for training on the Boeing 747 Model 400 aircraft simulator.

8-3543-15   3543-15

declassified by: UC, CTLU1, OGC, FBI
On: 03/01/2006

Part of FBI agent Harry Samit's memo, written to "advise the Federal Aviation Administration of a potential threat to the security of commercial aircraft."

suspicions. A company salesman there told him to leave Moussaoui alone—he was a paying customer. But the staff members at the flight academy were still worried. On their own, two of them contacted the Federal Bureau of Investigation. "I'm calling on a customer," one of them told an agent in the FBI's Minneapolis office. "If I'm wrong, it's probably going to cost me my job," he said, but he added, "I'd rather call and be wrong than not call and be right."

Within hours FBI agents appeared at the flight academy, asking its staff more questions about Moussaoui. The agents found that Moussaoui, a French citizen, had stayed in America longer than the time permitted by his visa, and on August 16, FBI agent Harry Samit arrested Moussaoui on an immigration violation.

The agents at the Minneapolis office of the FBI were concerned about something more serious than an immigration irregularity. They believed that Moussaoui might be a terrorist planning to hijack a plane. One of the flight instructors at Eagan had pointed out to them that a 747, with all its jet fuel, would make a powerful bomb.

Under questioning, Moussaoui stuck to the story he had told at the flight academy—he thought it would be amusing to learn how to fly a big commercial passenger jet. He refused to permit law enforcement officials to search his hotel room and his belongings, and they could not do so against his will unless they had a search warrant.

Samit, and another FBI agent, Coleen Rawley, each tried and failed to get warrants to search Moussaoui's room and belongings. An application for a criminal search warrant was turned down by FBI headquarters on the grounds that there wasn't enough evidence that a crime had been committed. Another application for a warrant, under the Foreign Intelligence Surveillance Act of 1978 (fiSA), was turned down because Moussaoui was not a known member of any terrorist organization. It is possible that this warrant might have been granted if Samit and Rawley's immediate superiors had been more cooperative. Later, both agents were highly critical of their bosses, and no wonder. After the terrorist attacks of September 11, 2001, Indiana senator Chuck Grassley would write to FBI director Robert Mueller:

If the application for the FISA warrant had gone forward, agents would have found information in Moussaoui's belongings that linked him both to a major financier of the hijacking plot working out of Germany, and to a Malaysian al-Qaida boss who had met with at least two other hijackers while under surveillance by intelligence officials.

Al Qaeda, also spelled Al-Qaida, is the name of the terrorist group headed by Osama bin Laden. At the time of Moussaoui's arrest, in addition to many other acts of terrorism around the world, Al Qaeda counted as major accomplishments the simultaneous attacks on the U.S. embassies in Kenya and Tanzania in 1998, which killed more than 220 people. FBI agent Harry Samit prepared a memo to the Federal Aviation Administration (FAA), the U.S. agency in charge of aircraft and flight safety, alerting officials to the possibility that terrorists might hijack planes in the near future—it seemed to Samit that Moussaoui might be part of a larger conspiracy and that there might be other hijackers out there. But Samit's superior at the FBI prevented Samit from sending the memo. Desperate to get the word out, Samit relied on his personal contacts and met with an official at the FAA. But the official failed to act on the information.

Finally, on September 12, 2001, a warrant to search Moussaoui's room and belongings came through. Found among his possessions were two knives, fighting gloves and shin guards, and a notebook containing the German phone number and the alias of Ramzi bin al-Shibh, the paymaster of a group of Al Qaeda terrorists who, it was learned too late, were planning to hijack airplanes.

SEPTEMBER 11, 2001

On September 11, 2001—the day before the search warrant was granted— nineteen Arab men, all Islamic extremists connected with Al Qaeda, hijacked four airplanes and attacked major American landmarks, killing thousands of innocent people. The hijackers had taken control of the four planes almost simultaneously. A later investigation found that three of the planes each had five hijackers aboard, but one had only four.

United Airlines Flight 175 was flown into the south tower of the World Trade Center in New York City. American Airlines Flight 11 was flown into the north tower. American Airlines Flight 77 smashed into the Pentagon. United Airlines Flight 93, the plane with only four hijackers, was still in the air when the other planes had reached their targets. Some of its passengers learned through their cell phones about the attacks on the World Trade Center and Pentagon and apparently realized that they could hope to survive only if they somehow managed to take control of the aircraft. This they attempted to do, rushing the hijackers and overcoming them. However, rather than give up the plane, the hijackers in the cockpit turned it upside down and headed toward the ground.

Wreckage of the World Trade Center.

Pictures of the missing cover a mailbox in New York City after the September 11 attacks.

The aircraft, which the terrorists probably intended to crash into the Capitol or the White House in Washington, DC, instead crashed into a Pennsylvania field, resulting in the deaths of everyone on board.

Nearly three thousand people died in the attacks, which, taken together, were the largest and most elaborate act of terrorism in history—and the most successful. Terrorists want publicity. They want to evoke a powerful reaction in as many people as possible, and according to that standard, no one could dispute the success of these attacks. The horrors of September 11 were endlessly replayed on news programs around the world. The ideology of the terrorists became an international obsession. Before long, people were referring to the attacks simply by their date—September 11 or just 9/11.

Though it is always a fiction to speak of a country as if it is a person with a single set of feelings and thoughts, for a while after the attacks this fiction was much closer to truth than it usually is. Television comics were stunned into sobriety. Media commentators, noting the cynical tone that had characterized American culture in the 1990s, began to say that from this day forward, irony was dead. It did not take long, however, for unfolding events to prove how wrong the analysts were on that score.

As people across the United States tried to come to grips with what had happened, the effort to uncover the full story of the crime began. The passenger lists of the four planes led investigators backwards along the trail of evidence that U.S. law enforcement and intelligence agencies had failed to uncover—credit card purchases and checks and names recorded on hotel registers, warnings from foreign police that this or that man thought to be connected with a terrorist group might be in the United States, and all the other "dots" that U.S. agencies had previously failed to connect.

Investigation of Zacarias Moussaoui turned up similarities between his past behavior and the past behavior of the hijackers. Like them, Moussaoui had been drawn into an extreme version of Islamic Fundamentalism, a worldwide movement that seeks to establish Islamic states—states run according to strict Islamic law—in countries where the majority of the population are Muslims. Not all Islamic Fundamentalists believe the same thing; not all approve of terrorism, and neither are all Islamic Fundamentalists hostile to the United States. The group to which Moussaoui and the September 11 hijackers belonged viewed the United States as the enemy of God and considered any action taken against it to be justified.

Like Moussaoui, at least six of the hijackers had trained on flight simulators at U.S. flight schools, most of them in 2000 and 2001. Mohammed Atta, the operational leader of the hijackers, who piloted the plane that hit the north tower of the World Trade Center, contacted thirty-one flight schools prior to his arrival in the United States, apparently checking them out to see which would be suitable for Al Qaeda's needs (he ultimately trained, with another hijacker, at Huffman Aviation in Venice, Florida). The 9/11 hijackers had also attended Al Qaeda training camps in Afghanistan. So, too, had Moussaoui.

Moussaoui had other connections with the hijackers: In September 2000, he had visited Malaysia and stayed in a condominium where two of the September 11 hijackers had lived earlier that year. Some of the money he spent in the United States apparently was sent to him from Hamburg, Germany, the location of a terrorist cell involved in the September 11 attacks. His computer disk contained information about crop-dusting, which the hijackers had considered to be a possible method for spreading deadly chemical or biological agents through the air.

The knives found among Moussaoui's belongings were similar to those purchased by the 9/11 hijackers.

However, there were also striking differences between Moussaoui and the hijackers. Each of the September 11 hijackers had been in direct contact with at least some of the others; Moussaoui had been alone. Their training had begun before his—some of them a year or more earlier. They had learned to pilot a plane; he had not. They blended in with their surroundings; he did not. Instead, Moussaoui had spoken and acted with extraordinary carelessness, not making a good effort to seem to be what he pretended to be. As a result, he had struck people as a strange man whose story did not add up; he had been arrested on an immigration violation before he could complete his mission, whatever it was.

The 9/11 Commission—an official investigative body that studied the attacks and the government failures that had allowed them to succeed—summed Moussaoui up as "an al-Qaeda mistake and a missed opportunity. An apparently unreliable operative, he had fallen into the hands of the FBI."

Protesters hold up a portrait of Osama bin Laden in Islamabad, Pakistan, during a rally on September 28, 2001, in support of Afghanistan's Taliban militia and against the United States. *Jehad,* also spelled *jihad,* means holy war in defense of Islam.

THE "TWENTIETH HIJACKER"

Within a few days of the attacks, Moussaoui's face appeared on the television news all over the world as the "twentieth hijacker"—the man who, because he had been arrested, had not been able to board Flight 93 and help perpetrate the September 11 attacks.

Moussaoui's mother, a retired employee of France's telephone company, said her son could not possibly be guilty of such a crime. He was a hard-working student. "How could he be involved in such a thing?" she said. "I cannot eat. I cannot sleep. I keep saying to myself, could this be? All my children, they each had their own rooms. They had pocket money. They went on vacations. I could understand if he had grown up unhappy or poor. But they had everything."

At the time of his arrest, Zacarias Moussaoui was thirty-three years old. His parents had come to France from Morocco, a former French colony, a few years before he was born. When he was young his mother moved to a shelter to escape abuse at the hands of her husband, who had been beating her and Zacarias's older sisters for years. Zacarias and the other children spent a year in an orphanage while their mother began to remake their lives. She found a job as a cleaning woman for the phone company, took night classes, passed a civil service test, and was promoted to a job in the phone company's mailroom.

When Zacarias was twelve, his mother moved the children to a small apartment in a town in the south of France, and two years later they moved to a pleasant villa in the town's suburbs. ("I wanted them to be away from the city and the drugs and all the trouble there," said his mother, soon after receiving the news of his arrest.) It was a quiet middle-class neighborhood of well-trimmed lawns. A block away from their house in one direction was a small park with benches and walking paths. A few blocks in the other direction was a nightclub that did not admit Arabs.

Official records of Moussaoui as a child give little clue as to the angry fanatic he would later become. As a teenager, he didn't get into trouble with the law. He loved sports. His high school records describe him as "a likeable boy, tenacious, a

Zacarias Moussaoui's mother, Aicha, holding a picture of her son.

slow worker but full of good will." On the other hand, as the defense at his trial would later point out, there was tragedy just beneath the surface: his father's violence, his year in an orphanage, the contempt he encountered as a dark-skinned Arab living in France. Mental illness ran in Moussaoui's family: both of his sisters had attempted suicide, and both had been diagnosed with schizophrenia, a serious psychiatric disorder from which Moussaoui may also suffer.

Although Moussaoui was a Muslim, his upbringing was not religious. Talking to reporters in France, his mother attributed Moussaoui's turn toward Islamic Fundamentalism to the visit of a female cousin with traditional Islamic views. In the family's house in Narbonne, all the children, boys and girls, had to make their beds, vacuum, and help with the dishes. The cousin told Zacarias and his older brother that this was women's work. "She told them that they were not acting like men," his mother recalled. "She told them that Muslim men should have four wives. She started criticizing me because I did not wear a veil. The boys liked what they heard."

Moussaoui received technical degrees from high school and a vocational college. After passing entrance examinations that qualified him for a government scholarship, he studied engineering. He worked for a while as a supervisor in a secondary school in Narbonne. He also studied English, and in 1991, when he was twenty-three, he went to England, planning to get a business degree. Moussaoui became involved with radical Islamists when he visited London's Finsbury Park mosque, a place where Islamic extremist groups find many of their recruits.

The methods used at places like the Finsbury Park mosque resemble the recruitment process of religious cults: The targets are young people who are far from home or estranged from their families. They are welcomed into the group, made to feel important, and indoctrinated into a special worldview with a series of lectures. The lectures work on their emotions and provide them with the key to history—a simple explanation for absolutely everything.

People like Moussaoui, who are from irreligious families, may be especially vulnerable to this kind of indoctrination; they have no deep convictions of their own to compete with the convictions of their recruiters. For the first time in their lives, they know what it is to have all the answers. Their new friends discourage them from engaging in dialogue with outsiders—they tell them the vast majority of mankind is deeply misguided—and warn them that people who try to change their minds must be avoided. No longer drifters lacking a sense of purpose, the young recruits have become superior people, people who know the hidden truth, people with a mission. Eventually, they are urged to cut off all contact with their families—as Moussaoui did in 1995—and are groomed for special services to the cause.

Moussaoui returned to France often enough to catch the eye of a French antiterrorist task force that saw him in the company of Islamic extremists whom they were tracking in 1996. In 1998, he attended a terrorist training camp in Afghanistan. Afghanistan was then under the control of an extreme Islamic Fundamentalist government called the Taliban, which had given shelter to Al Qaeda and its leader, Osama bin Laden. In September 2000, Moussaoui visited Malaysia and stayed at a condominum where other September 11 hijackers had stayed. From February 26 to May 29, 2001, Moussaoui took flying lessons at Airman Flight School in Norman, Oklahoma. He did not pass the course and left the school without a pilot's license. In early August, he received fourteen thousand dollars in wire transfers originating from Hamburg, Germany. This money probably helped him pay for the flight training at the Pan-Am International Flight Academy in Eagan, Minnesota, where he was arrested.

MILITARY TRIBUNAL OR CRIMINAL TRIAL?

In November 2001, a debate was going on within the U.S. Justice Department. Officials were trying to decide how to try Zacarias Moussaoui. Should he be tried by a civilian court or by military tribunal?

By this time, U.S. forces were in Afghanistan, fighting the Taliban. President George W. Bush had signed an executive order authorizing the use of military tribunals for foreigners charged with terrorism. Traditionally, military tribunals are conducted in battle zones where military personnel must do the work ordinarily done by the courts. This was obviously not the Bush administration's reason for wanting to try the terrorists by military tribunals. The reason was probably that military tribunals generally make it easier to convict suspects while maintaining the secrecy important to the newly declared "War on Terror." Defendants in military tribunals have fewer rights than defendants in regular criminal trials. In a trial by military tribunal, the government does not have to supply the defense with sensitive information just because it would help with the defendant's case.

The United States was facing this same decision—civilian court or military tribunal—with the Taliban prisoners captured in Afghanistan. The government ended up making the decision not to try them at first—officials responsible for preventing future attacks decided to lock them up indefinitely while squeezing them for information about Al Qaeda. Declaring that the prisoners were "unlawful combatants" not entitled to the protections of the Geneva Convention, the Bush administration brought most of them to a U.S. base in Guantánamo Bay, Cuba, a location the U.S. government considered to be outside U.S. law and perhaps outside all law—"the legal equivalent of outer space." The prisoners were kept there under conditions of unusual secrecy and subjected to repeated interrogations. In the five years following their capture, trials were set for around ten of the five-hundred-odd prisoners at Guantánamo Bay. As of 2007, no trials had

In this handout photo from the Department of Defense, Taliban and Al Qaeda detainees in orange jumpsuits sit in a holding area under the watchful eyes of military police at Camp X-Ray at Naval Base Guantánamo Bay, Cuba, during in-processing to the temporary detention facility on January 11, 2002.

actually taken place. The treatment of the prisoners at Guantánamo Bay has generated intense controversy, within the United States and around the world.

By the time of Zacarias Moussaoui's trial, other countries cooperating with America's War on Terror had captured and handed over high-ranking Al Qaeda members involved in the planning and financing of the September 11 attacks. As this book went to press, none of these prisoners, as with those interned at Guantánamo Bay, has received a trial.

Only Moussaoui has received one, and in fact, he received a regular civilian criminal trial in which his rights were meticulously respected. Why did Moussaoui get a trial when the others did not? This question will be debated for a long time to come. The answer may go something like this: The American public wanted contradictory things. On the one hand, they wanted to be protected; on the other hand, they wanted to see somebody prosecuted for the attacks of 9/11. To accomplish either of these goals, the government might have to undermine its efforts to achieve the other one. As the would-be hijacker in police custody before September 11, Moussaoui was more well known to the American public than were the Al Qaeda members handed to the United States by the police of other countries. At the same time, as a relatively low-ranking member of Al Qaeda, he was not especially valuable as a source of further information to the government. Unlike Moussaoui, the other captured Al Qaeda members knew secrets that if revealed could prevent future attacks. They might not reveal these secrets if they were treated as civilian criminal defendants, or even as prisoners of war under international law. And in interrogating these prisoners, perhaps using torture, which is illegal, the United States government may have made it impossible to convict them. The illegal treatment these prisoners have received might by itself result in their release if they were tried in civilian court. Furthermore, the revelations of their treatment could embarrass the United States government. The American officials in power at the time the torture occurred might even lose their jobs.

It would not be accurate to call Moussaoui a mere scapegoat, because he was certainly part of a terrorist plot. But he was not the most important member of the plot in custody. He was simply the one the U.S. government could afford to try in civilian court.

The indictment handed down against Moussaoui on December 11, 2001, detailed all that was known at the time of the conspiracy that led to the attacks of September 11, 2001. It accused Moussaoui of "conspiring with Osama bin Laden and Al Qaeda to murder thousands of innocent people in New York, Virginia and Pennsylvania on Sept. 11." Specifically, Moussaoui was charged with conspiracy to commit acts of terrorism, to commit aircraft piracy, to destroy aircraft, to use airplanes as weapons of mass destruction, to murder government employees, and to destroy property.

Since the crimes of which Moussaoui was accused of assisting had been committed in more than one place—in New York, Pennsylvania, and Virginia—the

U.S. Justice Department had a choice of locations in which to hold the trial. It chose Virginia, a conservative state, where jurors tended to favor the death penalty.

THE JUDGE AND THE LEGAL DEFENSE TEAM

The judge chosen to try the case, Leonie M. Brinkema, was a liberal appointed during the first term of President Bill Clinton, and she often angered conservatives with her decisions. When Clinton was running for reelection in 1996, his opponent Bob Dole cited Brinkema as a bad appointment and said she belonged in a judicial "hall of shame." On the other hand, lawyers who had appeared before her said that she was a fair judge, favoring neither the defense nor the prosecution, and that she exercised firm control over her courtroom. These qualities were about to be tested, for Judge Brinkema faced a complex case and a difficult defendant.

Since terrorist cells were not wiring money to Zacarias Moussaoui anymore, his defense would be paid for by American taxpayers. The court appointed a team of three lawyers to defend him. Since it was important that Moussaoui get a fair trial—and be seen getting a fair trial—the court appointed talented, highly competent lawyers. The team was headed by Frank W. Durham, Jr., who was used to handling cases that got a lot of attention from the media. He had previously represented W. Mark Felt, the former FBI assistant director found guilty of conspiring to violate the rights of leftist radicals in the 1970s by illegally searching their homes. Another team member, Gerald Zerkin, was a leading specialist in death-penalty cases. The third member, Edward B. McMahon, was an experienced civil and criminal courtroom lawyer. All three were morally and professionally committed to giving their unpopular client the best defense they could.

Zacarias Moussaoui was apparently not capable of understanding this. In the mental prison he had inhabited since long before his arrest, there was no such thing as an honorable enemy. He could not understand that people who did not share his beliefs, people who may even have despised him, would use all their skills to save his life.

MOUSSAOUI FIRES HIS DEFENSE TEAM

The Virginia federal circuit court in which Zacarias Moussaoui was to be tried was informally known as the "rocket docket" because of the speed with which cases that were heard there were handled. Moussaoui's trial would prove to be an exception to this rule, dragging on for four and a half years, most of them spent outside the courtroom in a battle of legal papers filed by the prosecution and the defense. The two sides would contend especially over the government's use of secret information and Moussaoui's insistence that he be allowed to call captured Al Qaeda leaders as witnesses for his defense.

At his pretrial hearing on January 2, 2002, Moussaoui was asked how he would plead. "In the name of Allah, I do not have anything to plead," said the defendant in heavily accented English. "I enter no plea. Thank you very much."

The judge decided to interpret this as a plea of not guilty, and went on to schedule a series of other pretrial hearings that would set up the ground rules of the trial, set to begin in the fall of that year.

The trial took its first unexpected turn a few weeks later on January 23, 2002, at a hearing where a defiant Moussaoui took it upon himself to dismiss his lawyers. Moussaoui said that he prayed to Allah for the "the destruction of the United States of America" and for the "destruction of the Jewish people and state." (In common with many other Islamic Fundamentalists, Moussaoui believed that America was under the control of an international Jewish conspiracy and conducted its foreign policy on behalf of Israel.)

Pointing to his lawyers, he said: "They have no understanding of terrorism, Muslims, mujahadeen." (*Mujahadeen* are "holy warriors," fighting in the name of Islam.) "I believe they are experienced. They are experienced in deception." He said that they were motivated by "greed, fame and vanity." He claimed that his trial was a struggle between a man willing to die for his religious beliefs and a group of "pagans, Jews, Christians, and hypocrites." He described himself repeatedly as "the slave of Allah." He said the U.S. government was "spending millions of their evil money to kill [him]," and asserted that Judge Brinkema herself was part of the plot—she was "here as a field general entrusted to get this matter over with quickly," and she took orders from President Bush.

It sounded as if Moussaoui was begging to be executed, but he stood by his not-guilty plea, reminding the judge that he was "innocent until proven guilty."

Judge Brinkema was in a difficult position, attempting to give a fair trial to a man who insisted on making bad choices. Should she force him to protect himself? She relied on precedent (what had been done before). In the past, non-lawyers who insisted on acting as their own legal counsel had been permitted to do so, provided they were sane, so she told Moussaoui that she would allow him to be his own lawyer if a psychiatrist examined him and said he was not mentally ill. But at the same time she urged him to let the court-appointed lawyers do their job and said that she would keep them on hand as backup in case he turned out to be incapable of defending himself. "You're obviously a very smart man and you're able to read American law books and glean from some of the rulings, but I have to tell you that the American legal system is complicated," she said. "I am not going to permit you to be in a court of law without any legal sources whatsoever."

Months of wrangling followed between the judge and Moussaoui, who refused to be examined by a psychiatrist (saying he would "not participate in an obscene Jewish science"). Finally he agreed to submit to a two-hour psychiatric examination, which concluded that he was sane. The defense team, however, had hired two psychologists who had serious doubts about Moussaoui's sanity. But since Moussaoui had refused to meet with them, their opinions had to be based on secondhand reports of his behavior, and Brinkema found them unconvincing.

MOUSSAOUI ASKS TO INTERVIEW AL QAEDA MEMBERS

Moussaoui officially became his own counsel at a hearing on June 13, 2002. He remained in charge of his own case until November 2003. At this time, Judge Brinkema, saying that he had violated her orders by filing "frivolous, scandalous, disrespectful or repetitive" court papers, reinstated his original defense team.

During the seventeen months that Moussaoui acted as his own lawyer, he did many things that were strange and some that made good legal sense. On the strange side were the majority of his legal motions to the court, full of slurs on the United States, the Jews, his long-suffering lawyers and the judge, and various people in the news. On the other side, Moussaoui did file some useful motions to the court, demanding evidence from terrorists that would cast doubt on his involvement in the September 11 attacks.

In fall of 2002, one of the plot's organizers, Ramza bin al-Shibh, was captured in Pakistan and turned over to American custody. Moussaoui filed motions asking to call al-Shibh as a witness. Since al-Shibh had been named by the prosecutors as a planner of the conspiracy in which Moussaoui had been accused of participating—and his name and phone number had been found in a notebook of Moussaoui's seized by the FBI after fighting so hard for a search warrant—there was no disputing his relevance as a witness. Moussaoui was entitled to interview—or gain access to prior interrogations of—anyone who might provide evidence of his innocence.

Ramz Bin Al-shibh, named by Zacarias Moussaoui's prosecutors as a mastermind of the conspiracy in which Moussaoui participated.

Moussaoui's request put prosecutors in an awkward position. The Defense Department and the Central Intelligence Agency were refusing to make al-Shibh and other captured Al Qaeda figures available for defense interviews. The reasons for this reluctance may have been the same ones that had prevented these men from being brought to trial. They were being held in secret locations, perhaps illegally. Interviews with them might reveal secrets that could damage the fight against terrorism or the reputation of the United States and the Bush administration. But if Shibh wasn't allowed to testify, the government's case against Moussaoui could fall apart on the grounds that the courts could not give him a fair trial. Despite this danger, the prosecution tried to avoid turning over the results of the government's interrogation of al-Shibh.

In spring of 2003, the news media learned from leaks that other captured Al Qaeda leaders had said in interrogations that Moussaoui was not involved in the 9/11 plot and that (as Moussaoui himself claimed) he had been sent on a different terrorist mission. Judge Brinkema ordered the Justice Department to turn over any information in its possession that might be evidence of Moussaoui's innocence. She ordered that Moussaoui be allowed to interview the captured Al Qaeda leaders involved in the September 11 plot. The government strongly objected.

For nearly a year and a half, the Moussaoui trial was delayed as appeals courts decided what to do about this dilemma. In a compromise between the claims of national security and Moussaoui's right to a fair trial, the U.S. Court of Appeals of the Fourth Circuit ordered that he be permitted to submit written questions to the high-ranking captured Al Qaeda members. The case was further delayed while the government appealed this decision to the Supreme Court, which announced in March 2005 that it would not hear the case—in effect upholding the decision of the circuit court. By this time, Moussaoui's court-appointed lawyers were once again officially handling his defense. He was no more cooperative with them this time than he had been before.

MOUSSAOUI PLEADS GUILTY

All the wrangling over Moussaoui's right to question the Al Qaeda prisoners became moot when, unpredictable as ever, he changed his plea to guilty. On April 22, 2005, standing before the judge in the dark green jump suit provided for him by the United States government, Moussaoui said, "I came to the United States of America to be part, O.K., of a conspiracy to use airplane as a weapon of mass destruction."

He did not quite admit to the specific acts of which he had been accused, however. He denied that he had been part of a conspiracy to implement the attacks of September 11, and he did not admit to being the "twentieth hijacker," meant for Flight 93. Instead, Moussaoui claimed that he was part of a plan to force the release of sheik Omar Abdel Rahman, a blind Muslim scholar serving a life sentence for conspiracy to blow up New York bridges, tunnels, and other landmarks in 1993. "I am guilty of a broad conspiracy to use a weapon of mass destruction to destroy the White House," said Moussaoui. He empha-

Omar Abdel Rahman, serving a life sentence in the Butner Medical Center in Butner, North Carolina.

sized that he had not admitted to any connection with the 9/11 attacks.

With Moussaoui's guilty plea, the long-awaited trial that was meant to determine the facts of the case was bypassed and another trial to determine Moussaoui's sentence began. The government was seeking the death penalty.

JURY SELECTION

Because there was no trial to determine guilt, the prosecution would use the sentencing trial to establish Moussaoui's connection to the September 11 attacks. They would maintain that, at the very least, Moussaoui knew of the planned attacks and could have prevented them by telling what he knew when he was being questioned in August 2001 by the FBI. The defense would try to prove that Moussaoui's lies to FBI investigators had made no difference. They would contend that the government had already been given more information concerning the upcoming attacks than Moussaoui could have provided. Their approach to the case had a special interest for the American public apart from the question of Moussaoui's guilt or innocence, since they intended to expose the U.S. government failures that had enabled the terrorists to be successful.

Judge Brinkema set aside the month of February 2006 for jury selection in the sentencing trial; this was an unusually long time because it would be difficult to find people who could honestly say they had not already made up their minds. The jury was selected from a pool of five hundred candidates. At a preliminary screening, they each filled out a forty-four-page questionnaire prepared by Judge Brinkema, asking them for their opinions about Muslims from North Africa and

In an artist's rendering, Zacarias Moussaoui, with beard, argues before U.S. District Judge Leonie M. Brinkema, seated back, during a pretrial hearing. The men seated in the front of the picture are Moussaoui's lawyers. The men standing on the right and left are security.

whether they knew anyone killed in the September 11 attacks. Every member of the jury would have to be, in the jargon of criminal lawyers, "death qualified"— someone who could swear that he or she would be willing to impose the death penalty if it was justified in this case.

The potential jurors were divided into four large groups; one at a time, each group was brought into the spectators' section of the courtroom to be addressed by Judge Brinkema, who told them that they faced "an awesome responsibility."

Moussaoui, after looking over the first group of jurors from his place in the center of the courtroom, shouted, "I won't be heard by this court," and then gestured to his court-appointed lawyers, saying, "These lawyers are not my lawyers." Brinkema ordered that he be removed from the courtroom. As he was escorted out, he placed his hand on his head, indicating that he was not resisting, and then said loudly, "I am Al Qaeda. I'm the enemy. This trial is a circus." Moussaoui was brought in again to see each new group of potential jurors, and each time he shouted at them and was ejected from the courtroom.

At a special hearing, Brinkema ordered that he be barred from the courtroom during the remainder of jury selection. As he was led from the courtroom, he shouted, "God curse America." The next day, however, he was back in the courtroom, apparently having promised Judge Brinkema that he would behave himself. And so he did, as the jury pool was gradually whittled down to the required twelve.

THE DEATH-PENALTY TRIAL BEGINS

The death-penalty trial of Zacarias Moussaoui would have two phases: The members of the jury would first hear evidence to help them decide whether Moussaoui was eligible for the death penalty. Then (if they deemed him eligible) they would hear evidence to help them decide if he should receive it.

Arrangements were made for more than five hundred relatives of 9/11 victims to watch the proceedings on closed-circuit televisions in courthouses in Long Island, Boston, Philadelphia, Newark, and Manhattan, as well as in another room of the same building in Alexandria, Virginia, where the trial was taking place.

There were also a dozen seats reserved in the courtroom for relatives of those killed—those who wanted to would be allowed to occupy them on a rotating basis. The feelings of these people were varied—some were hoping for a scrap of justice, some simply wanted to understand what could make people do such things, and some were not certain what they wanted but were inwardly compelled to watch anything that had to do with the 9/11 attacks.

In the first week of March 2006, the prosecution began presenting its case. It introduced a videotaped interview that it had conducted in 2002 with Fauzi Bafana, former treasurer of Jamaah Islamiyah, a Southeast Asian terrorist group linked to Al Qaeda. In the interview, Bafana, who had been arrested in November 2002, testified that Moussaoui had asked him for financial help in achieving his goal of flying an airplane into the White House. Since the interview had been done when Moussaoui was acting as his own lawyer, the four-hour videotape included Moussaoui's cross-examination of Bafana.

Michael Maltbie - Re: The FISA Quest   Page

DEFEND
EXHII
35
U.S. v. Mou
Cr. No. 01-

From: RAY MORROW
To: Michael Maltbie
Date: Tue, Aug 28, 2001 3:56 PM
Subject: Re: The FISA Quest

Mike - Thanks for your help and continued support.

Thanks
Ray

>>> Michael Maltbie 08/28/01 01:56PM >>>
Ray, Greg:

We just left a meeting w/ Spike Bowman, #1 in NSLU. He says that we have even less that I thought. Apparently, even if we could show that the ZM that recruited ▮▮▮ in France is the one you have locked up in INS detention, we still don't have a connection to a foreign power. We would need intel to indicate the guy was actually a part of the group, an integral part of the movement or organization, and not just an individual that told a brother how he could serve Allah.

Greg: Give me a call and we will talk about what to do next. As I said yesterday, you all did a great job to i.d., interview, and neutralize this guy. There are a couple more things we can still do -- w/ the assistance of our LEGATs.

Mike

Memo from FBI agent Ray Morrow, regarding his attempt to gain permission to search Zacarias Moussaoui's belongings.

The government next presented live witnesses. Harry Samit, the FBI agent from Minnesota, told of his attempts to get a warrant to search Moussaoui's belongings. He testified that Moussaoui's lies had sent him on "wild goose chases" in the days before the attacks. This was important for the government's contention that Moussaoui's deceptions had caused the deaths of innocent people on September 11—if Moussaoui had said he belonged to Al Qaeda and planned to fly planes into landmarks, an intense investigation would have followed that might have prevented the attacks. Then the prosecution put on Moussaoui's flight instructor from Eagan, who talked of his suspicions about Moussaoui.

JUDGE BRINKEMA HALTS THE TRIAL

At the beginning of the following week, Judge Brinkema learned from the prosecution that some of the government's upcoming witnesses had been improperly coached. Carla A. Martin, a lawyer for the Transportation Security Administration, had given portions of the previous week's trial proceedings to seven witnesses who had yet to testify. By doing so, Martin was violating a court order. Judge Brinkema had earlier ruled that most witnesses could not attend or follow the trial and could not read the transcripts, because she did not want them to be influenced by the other witnesses' testimony. In e-mail messages, the lawyer seemed to tell some of the witnesses how they should testify to support the prosecution's argument that Moussaoui bore some responsibility for the deaths caused by the September 11 attacks. Furious, Brinkema called a halt to the proceedings. She said that she was considering ending the trial and declaring Moussaoui ineligible for the death penalty. "In all my years on the bench, I've never seen a more egregious violation of the rule about witnesses."

Though the defense argued that Brinkema should indeed end the death-penalty case and impose a sentence of life imprisonment on Moussaoui, the judge instead disqualified the aviation officials who had been tampered with as witnesses. The trial moved forward.

MORE PROCEEDINGS

When the FBI agents called by the prosecution were cross-examined by the defense, Moussaoui's attorneys found it easy to bring out the agents' frustration at the way their superiors handled the investigation. Thus, their testimony cast doubt on Moussaoui's responsibility for 9/11—perhaps even if he had told them what Al Qaeda had planned, they wouldn't have been able to act quickly enough to prevent it. The stubbornness of their superiors would have made it impossible for them to make use of the information.

The prosecution's last few witnesses were more effective. People in charge of security at the Federal Aviation Administration testified that if the FBI had officially alerted them of an impending attack—an official alert would have been given if Moussaoui had told the truth to investigators—the FAA would have stepped up security measures. They would have banned all knives on flights, made metal detectors more sensitive, and ordered physical searches of passengers. The prosecution rested after these witnesses.

Next it was time for the defense lawyers to put on their case. They were expected to present exhibits—such as recorded testimony of captured Al Qaeda leaders—to establish that Moussaoui did not know enough about the 9/11 plot to have helped the FBI stop it. The defense team would also emphasize the FBI's incompetence in order to suggest that the agents wouldn't have used the information anyway, even if they had had it.

Before the defense lawyers could do these things, however, their client insisted on testifying. Moussaoui did everything he could to hurt his case. He gave a detailed account of his involvement with the 9/11 plot, insisting that he knew the other hijackers and was to have been involved with the attack on the day it occurred. He said that he and Richard Reid (the "shoe bomber" who was arrested on December 22, 2001, when he tried to blow up a passenger jet by igniting explosives hidden in his shoes) were going to fly a plane into the White House on September 11, 2001. When cross-examined, Moussaoui affirmed the exact point

that the prosecution wanted to establish in this part of the death-penalty trial—
he said he had known of the 9/11 plot and lied to help it go forward.

The defense did its best to undo the damage Moussaoui had done to his own
case. One lawyer read out loud a written statement by captured Al Qaeda member Khalid Sheikh Mohammed, the planner of the September 11 attacks, who
was being held overseas in a secret location by the Central Intelligence Agency.
This statement contradicted Moussaoui's confession. According to Mohammed,
Moussaoui was not a part of the 9/11 plot but rather a fringe figure who might
have been used in a second wave of attacks. The next day the defense read testimony from other captured Al Qaeda organizers, who said that Moussaoui had
never been part of the September 11 attacks. "He had dreams about flying a plane
into the White House," said a South Asian terrorist known as Hambali, who was
captured in 2003. According to Hambali, Moussaoui was known to be "not right
in the head and having a bad character."

The defense also played a videotape of the testimony that Thomas J. Pickard,
acting director of the FBI at the time of the attacks, had given to the National
Commission on Terrorist Attacks on April 13, 2004. Pickard had been asked
what he would have done if, prior to the attacks, he had known the following
three facts: Zacarias Moussaoui was an Islamic extremist taking flying lessons,

Four terrorism suspects held in secret locations at the time of the Moussaoui trial. From left, Khalid Sheik
Mohammed, believed to be the planner of the September 11 attacks; Ramzi Bin Al-shibh, an alleged would-be
9/11 hijacker; Abu Zubaydah, who was believed to be a link between Osama bin Laden and many Al Qaeda cells
before he was captured in Pakistan in 2002; and Riduan Isamuddin, known as Hambali, who was suspected of
being the mastermind of a string of deadly bomb attacks in Indonesia. The four were later moved to the naval
base in Guantánamo Bay.

two identified Al Qaeda terrorists were probably in the country in August 2001, and an FBI agent in Phoenix had drafted a memorandum saying that he noticed that an unusual number of young Middle Eastern men were enrolling in American flight schools and thought they might be planning some hijacking plot. Pickard had reminded the commission that the FBI had been evaluating thousands of leads in the summer of 2001. "I don't know, with all the information the FBI collects, whether we would have had the ability to hone in specifically on those three items."

As the case wound up on March 29, 2006, the prosecutors maintained that Zacarias Moussaoui had used Al Qaeda training to deceive the FBI. "Zacarias Moussaoui came to this country to kill as many Americans as he could," said a prosecution lawyer. His immigration arrest prevented him from killing them by hijacking an airplane. "So instead, he killed people by lying."

Edward B. MacMahon, Jr., speaking for the defense, had the task of undoing Moussaoui's testimony against himself. Clearly, said MacMahon, Moussaoui was exaggerating his involvement out of a desire for notoriety. "He was never slated, except in his dreams, to be part of the plot," MacMahon told the jury. "Now he wants to write a role for himself in history when the truth was he was an Al Qaeda hanger-on."

Moreover, the defense argued, there was no way of knowing whether the government could have thwarted the plot if Moussaoui had told what he knew. MacMahon pointed to the difficulties FBI agent Harry Samit had encountered in getting his superiors to act on the information he had obtained. Supposing Moussaoui had provided the FBI with a few more clues, that did not mean, said MacMahon, that the FBI "would have transformed itself into a flawless institution." He asked the jurors to disprove Moussaoui's belief that they would have him killed simply because they were Americans. "Show him we are not the hate-filled vengeful Americans Zacarias Moussaoui thinks you are."

The jurors deliberated for sixteen hours. They had to decide if Moussaoui met four criteria in making him eligible to receive the death penalty: (1) that he was over eighteen at the time of the crime, (2) he had deliberately taken an action that might lead to deaths, (3) he had done so planning that deaths would occur, and (4) at least one death actually had occurred because of his actions. Of these four issues, only one was in doubt—whether Moussaoui's actions had really led to the deaths of the 9/11 victims. When they returned to the courtroom on April 3, 2006, the jurors unanimously declared that the criteria had been met. Moussaoui was eligible for the death penalty.

The jury was unemotional as the verdict was read. Two of the victims' relatives in the courtroom quietly wiped away tears. As he left the courtroom, Moussaoui shouted, "You'll never get my blood!"

THE LAST PHASE

Moussaoui had not yet been sentenced to death—the jurors had merely determined that the criteria for the death penalty had been met. They had decided that Moussaoui was responsible for the deaths and had intended them. Now, in the next, final phase of the death-penalty trial, they were supposed to decide if his actions met a couple of other, less tangible criteria. In a way, they would be asked whom they pitied more, Moussaoui or the people who were said to be his victims.

The jurors would listen to witnesses who would help them make their decision, and they would use a form to guide them in their thinking. The form included a list of "aggravating factors" suggested by the prosecution, factors that would incline the jurors to vote for the death penalty. Among them were the horror surrounding the deaths, the grief of the victims' families, and the devastation caused to New York City. The form also included "mitigating factors" suggested by the defense. These were factors that might cause them to feel sorry for the defendant or suspect that he was not fully responsible for his actions—factors such as Moussaoui's unhappy childhood and the possibility that he might be mentally unbalanced.

As the death penalty trial moved into its final phase, most legal experts said that Moussaoui's fate was sealed. The jurors had already decided that Moussaoui was responsible for the deaths on 9/11. Given the number of the deaths and the horror of the circumstances, surely the jurors would decide that the aggravating factors far outweighed any mitigating factors.

The prosecution's first witness in the final phase of the trial was Rudolph Giuliani, who had been mayor of New York City at the time of the attacks. Sitting in the witness box beside a four-foot-high scale model of the World Trade Center, Giuliani described his reactions on that day and the days that followed. He told of seeing two people jump to their deaths from one of the burning towers while holding hands. "That image comes back to me every day."

When Giuliani was finished, the prosecution called relatives of victims to the witness stand, one after the other, each with a different tale of pain and loss. Jurors heard from a man whose daughter, an airline attendant, was on one of the planes that crashed into the World Trade Center. He had at first been told that she was not on the plane. The man described how his wife had retreated from life

Alice Hoagland, whose son Mark Bingham died on United Airlines Flight 93 on September 11, 2001, speaks to reporters in front of U.S. District Court in Alexandria, Virginia, after testifying for the defense in the sentencing trial of Zacarias Moussaoui. Hoagland said that she testified for the defense because her son loved all things living, and added, "We are all part of the human family . . . none of us are beyond redemption."

after their daughter's death and how his other daughter now slept only a few hours a night, and then only with the television on. Jurors heard from a New York City police officer whose wife, also a police officer, had died while helping to evacuate the south tower. A man from India told of his sister's suicide after her husband was killed aboard one of the hijacked planes. Altogether, thirty-five witnesses testified to their grief for loved ones lost as a result of the attacks.

The defense brought forward witnesses it hoped would persuade the jury to spare Moussaoui's life. A social worker who had spoken with Moussaoui's relatives, teachers, and doctors in France testified that Moussaoui's father, a former boxer, regularly beat Moussaoui's sisters and mother. His mother had often been beaten badly enough to need to go to a hospital, and Moussaoui had been put in orphanages because of the instability in his home. A psychologist who had seen Moussaoui in his cell testified that he had displayed classic schizophrenic symptoms and cast doubt on his confession.

In its most surprising move, the defense presented its own group of relatives of the victims of 9/11, twenty-four witnesses who testified to their pain and sorrow just as the witnesses for the prosecution had. These people were not asked what sentence they thought Moussaoui should receive (the prosecution witnesses had not been asked either), but the jury knew these witnesses were testifying for the defense.

THE VERDICT

The jury began deliberating on Zacarias Moussaoui's ultimate fate on Monday, April 25, 2006. They met as a group for forty-one hours over the course of seven days. On May 3, they confounded the experts by sentencing Moussaoui to life in prison without parole. The reasons they gave most often on the forms the judge had provided them were surprising to people who had been following the trials. According to what most of them had written, Moussaoui's difficult childhood had mattered more to the jurors than his obvious mental instability or his desire to be a martyr.

Moussaoui did not look particularly pleased as the verdict was read, but later, as he was led from the courtroom, he shouted, "America, you lost. I won!"

The handful of family members of 9/11 victims in the courtroom showed little emotion either toward the verdict or this typical outburst from Moussaoui. When these survivors and others were questioned by reporters later, their responses to the verdict varied. Many wished that Moussaoui had been sentenced to death but said they understood why the jury had come to its decision and declared their faith in the American judicial system. Several said they agreed that Moussaoui had been at most a bit player in the 9/11 attacks and that they hoped the prosecutions would not end with him. At the time, it seemed unlikely that they would get their wish.

In the Moussaoui case, the United States had bent over backwards to give a fair trial to a man who did not want one. But more important figures in the 9/11 attacks, held in secret prisons, have not been brought to trial at all and might never be brought to trial. The U.S. government wants information from these people more than it wants justice. Decisions to try them or not try them are being decided by considerations other than the law.

THE AFTERMATH

America moves into the twenty-first century facing the new devil of international terrorism, and with the country's legal traditions under stress as a result. The rules seem to be changing. Arrests that would have once led to trials have led instead to long imprisonments away from our shores. Lawyers working for the U.S. government have used their training to justify new sorts of trials, such as military tribunals in which defendants have fewer rights. These lawyers assure the American people that there is nothing really new in what they are doing and that we should not worry; these new rules will be used only against our enemies. They claim we need not worry that our own rights will be seriously eroded by the ruthlessness and secrecy entailed in a perpetual War on Terror. But on this question the jury is still out.

Justice.

Epilogue

LAW IN THE AGE OF TERROR

America's symbol of justice is a woman wearing a blindfold, holding balanced scales. We use it to remind ourselves that everyone is entitled to a fair trial, no matter how bad the crime or how hated the criminal.

We have not always lived up to this difficult ideal, but if we measure progress by the trials in this book, we have been getting better since our years as a British colony. None of the accused in the Salem witch trials in 1692 had lawyers; anyone who spoke up for them was liable to be called a witch. Two centuries later, the anarchists on trial for the Haymarket bombing were at least given the benefit of counsel.

By the twentieth century, the American justice system had made great strides. In 1925, John Thomas Scopes—an agent of the devil to small-town Fundamentalists—was defended by Clarence Darrow, one of the best trial lawyers of the century. In 1949, Alger Hiss, who was believed to be a Communist spy, received a fair trial despite the country's deep fear of Communism. Most recently, in 2006, the judge, the defense lawyers, and even the prosecutors involved in the trial of the accused terrorist Zacarias Moussaoui all shared a deep commitment to the idea that the accused in an American courtroom is entitled to the protections of the law.

Still, there will always be people who think that punishing criminals or defeating the enemy is more important than a fair trial. Such views are especially attractive during an emergency, such as the period that followed September 11, 2001. In 2007, Charles D. Stimson, the government official in charge of the suspected terrorists detained in Guantánamo Bay, said it was "shocking" that attorneys from the top law firms in the United States were representing the detained terrorists. Stimson, a lawyer himself, hinted that corporations that did business with these law firms ought to make it clear that they would not tolerate such a practice.

Stimson's words moved Karen J. Mathis, president of the American Bar Association, to remind him of what he ought to have learned in law school (if not in elementary school, middle school, or high school). "Lawyers," said Mathis, "represent people in criminal cases to fulfill a core American value: the treatment of all people equally before the law."

Witch, anarchist, atheist, Communist, terrorist—whatever form we decide the devil has taken, we deal fairly with him not for his sake, but for our own.

Glossary

anarchism: the theory or doctrine that all forms of government are oppressive and should be abolished.

appeal: to request that the outcome of a trial be reviewed and overturned by a higher court (an appeals court or appellate court).

appellate court: a court that corrects or confirms the decisions made in lower courts. The highest appellate court in the United States is the U.S. Supreme Court.

Armageddon: the scene of a final battle between the forces of good and evil, which according to biblical prophecy will occur at the end of the world.

blacklist: a list of people who are being denied a particular privilege, service, or mobility. Especially, a blacklist is a list of workers known to be union organizers which employers share among each other to suppress the growth of unions.

circuit court: state court that deals with cases in several counties or a district.

clemency: mercy.

commute: to change a punishment to a less severe one, as when a death sentence is commuted to life imprisonment.

constitutionality: whether a law is consistent with and permissible under the U.S. Constitution.

contempt of court: an act or omission that interferes with the orderly administration of justice, or that impairs the dignity of the court; usually punishable by a fine or imprisonment.

cross-examine: in a trial, to ask questions of a witness for the opposing side.

defendant: a person charged in a civil or criminal court case.

defense: the defendant and his or her team of lawyers; also, the plan that a defendant and the defense team have to refute the charges against him or her.

deposition: sworn, written testimony.

discovery: part of the pretrial litigation process during which each party requests relevant information and documents from the other side in an attempt to "discover" pertinent facts.

district court: a federal trial court sitting in each district of the United States.

expert witness: a witness who by virtue of education, profession, publication, or experience is believed to have special knowledge of a given subject beyond that of the average person, sufficient to give an opinion that others may officially and legally rely on.

expunged: erased, removed from the record.

Geneva Conventions: a series of international treaties concerning the laws of war; the rules deriving from those treaties.

grand jury: a jury that investigates accusations against persons charged with crimes, charged with the responsibility of indicting them for trial if there is sufficient evidence.

HUAC: The House Un-American Activities Committee, a congressional committee that conducted investigations and held hearings on subversive (anti-government) activities, especially Communism and espionage, during the 1940s and 1950s.

hung jury: a jury that cannot deliver a verdict because the jury members cannot reach a unanimous conclusion.

ideology: a system of political ideas.

indict: to formally charge with the commission of a crime.

jury: a group of people, usually twelve, sworn to hear evidence in a law case and to deliver a decision.

levy: to impose or collect, i.e., levy a fine.

lockout: the withholding of work from employees and closing down of a workplace by an employer during a labor dispute.

magistrate: a civil officer empowered to administer the law.

military tribunal: trial by military commission, or a panel of military judges, a form of trial sometimes conducted in time of war on the grounds that the normal machinery of justice has broken down.

militiaman: member of an army composed of ordinary citizens rather than professional soldiers.

minimum wage: the lowest wage that employers may legally pay their workers; prior to minimum wage laws there was no lowest legal wage.

motion: an application made to a court for an order or a ruling.

opinion: a written explanation that accompanies the ruling of a judge, especially the opinion of the judge in an appellate court.

perjury: the crime of lying under oath.

preliminary hearing: a preliminary examination of an accused person, usually one in which the accused is represented by a lawyer and a representative of the prosecution and judge is present.

prosecute: to initiate a civil or criminal court action against someone.

prosecuting attorney: a public official who conducts criminal proceedings on behalf of the state.

prosecution: the team of the prosecuting attorneys.

prosecutor: prosecuting attorney.

quash: an action by which a judge sets aside an order or nullifies an earlier action.

rest a case: to cease voluntarily the presentation of evidence: "The defense rests."

ruling: an official decision, especially by a judge.

scalawag: term of abuse used to describe a white Southerner who worked for or supported the federal government during the Reconstruction period after the American Civil War.

search warrant: a court order permitting law officers to search a person's home or belongings for evidence of a crime.

slander: oral communication of false statements injurious to a person's reputation.

socialism: a theory or system of social organization in which the means of producing and distributing goods is owned collectively or by a centralized government that plans and controls the economy.

social security: a government program that provides a pension to retired workers.

speakeasy: an illegal bar during the Prohibition Era (1920–33).

state's evidence: evidence for the prosecution in state or federal trials. Individuals suspected of a crime are said to "turn state's evidence" if they testify for the prosecution in exchange for a reduced sentence or other lenient treatment.

statute: a law.

statute of limitations: a law setting a time limit on legal action.

subpoena: an order for a person to appear in court.

test case: a legal action whose outcome is likely to set a precedent or test the constitutionality of a law.

testify: to give evidence under oath, especially in a trial.

testimony: declarations made under oath in a trial or in preliminary hearings leading up to a trial.

unemployment insurance: a government program under which employers are taxed to provide benefits to employees who lose their jobs through no fault of their own.

venue: the locality from which a jury is drawn and in which a case is tried.

verdict: the decision reached by a jury at the end of a trial.

welfare: financial or other aid provided, especially by the government, to people in need.

workmen's compensation: a government insurance program that provides money for workers injured on the job and for the dependents of workers killed on the job.

Notes

Chapter 1: The Salem Witch Trials

"Why do you thus torment these poor children?": Frances Hill, *A Delusion of Satan: The Full Story of the Salem Witch Trials* (New York: Doubleday, 1995), 46.

"We ourselves were not capable to understand": Claudia Durst Johnson and Vernon E. Johnson, *Understanding "The Crucible"* (Westport, CT: Greenwood Press, 1998), 115–16. The entire apology is reprinted in this collection of original documents from the trials.

"Whish! Whish!": Marion L. Starkey, *The Devil in Massachusetts* (New York: Alfred A. Knopf, 1949), 21–32. See Starkey's book for vivid descriptions of the early afflictions of the girls.

"The evil hand is upon them": Chadwick Hanson, *Witchcraft in Salem* (New York: George Braziller, 1969), 20.

For two hundred years *Maelleus Maleficarum*: Laurel Van Der Linde, *The Devil in Salem Village: The Story of the Salem Witchcraft Trials*. Spotlight on American History (Brookfield, CT: Millbrook Press, 1992), 18.

a prominent Boston minister named Increase Mather: Marilynne Roach, *In the Days of the Salem Witchcraft Trials* (Boston: Houghton Mifflin, 1996), 34. Father and son Increase and Cotton Mather were two key players in the events of 1692; for more written by them, see Mary Beth Norton, *In the Devil's Snare* (New York: Alfred A. Knopf, 2002), 34–35, 38–40.

The evil acts—the *maleficia*—of witches: Norton, *Devil's Snare*, 6–7.

"a city upon a hill": Kiernan Doherty, *Puritans, Pilgrims, and Merchants: Founders of the Northeastern Colonies* (Minneapolis: Oliver Press, 1999), 29. The complete quote follows: "For we must consider that we shall be as a city upon a hill, the eyes of all people are upon us; so that if we shall deal falsely with our God in this work we have undertaken and so cause him to withdraw present help from us, we shall be made a story and by word through the world we shall open the mouths of enemies to speak evil of the ways of God and all professors for God's sake; we shall shame the faces of many of God's servants and cause their prayers to be turned to curses until we are thrown out of the good land."

invited Samuel Parris to be its minister: Paul Boyer and Stephen Nissenbaum, *Salem Possessed: The Social Origins of Witchcraft* (Cambridge: Harvard University Press, 1976), 61–62. See this source for more on the conflict over separation between Salem Town and Salem Village.

A familiar of one of the accused witches was "a thing with a head like a woman with two leggs and wings": Norton, *Devil's Snare*, 28.

the Parrises' slave, Tituba, baked a "witch cake": Ibid., 20.

"[going] to the Devil for help against the Devil" and "The Devil hath been raised among us": Ibid.

Sarah Good was a sick, homeless beggar: Starkey, *Massachusetts*, 41. Starkey goes on to describe Osborne's many odd behaviors: "When asked why she didn't go to church, she answered, 'For want of cloose!' Whenever she was turned away from a house on her begging trips, she started muttering and cows often died afterward. When asked what she was muttering, she said it was the Commandments. She had called children vile names shortly before the girls in the Parris household fell ill. After she was dismissed [from the witness stand], she said, 'It is Gammer Osburne that doth pinch and afflict the children!'"

the egg white turned into the shape of a coffin: Carol F. Karlsen, *The Devil in the Shape of a Woman* (New York: Vintage Books, 1987), 36.

"a just warning to others to take heed of handling the Devil's weapons": Mark Aronson, *Witchhunt: Mysteries of the Salem Witch Trials* (New York: Atheneum Books for Young Readers, 2003), 59, and Norton, *Devil's Snare*, 24–26.

Modern ideas about the rights of the accused: Lawrence M. Friedman, *Crime and Punishment in American History* (New York: Basic Books, 1993), 45. Friedman includes the following excerpt from *The Laws and Liberties of Massachusetts of 1648* (a code of law that served as the basis for civil and criminal justice in Massachusetts). He quotes: "If any man or woman be a WITCH, that is, hath or consulteth with a familiar spirit, they shall be put to death." For more about the Salem witch trials from a legal perspective, see Peter Charles Hoffer, *The Salem Witch Trials: A Legal History* (Lawrence: University Press of Kansas, 1997).

Accompanied by marshals armed with spears: Hill, *Delusion*, 41.

Hathorne was the great-grandfather of Nathaniel Hawthorne: Ibid., 85. In an effort to disassociate himself from his great-grandfather, Nathaniel Hawthorne added a *w* to his name.

Once, on her way to be questioned, a supposed witch: Boyer and Nissenbaum, *Salem Possessed*, 15.

"Sarah Good," Hathorne asked: Paul Boyer and Stephen Nissenbaum, *The Salem Witchcraft Papers: Verbatim Transcripts of the Legal Documents of the Salem Witchcraft Outbreak of 1692*, vol. 2 (New York: Da Capo Press, 1977), 357–58. The University of Virginia maintains the legal documents from the Salem witch trials in electronic form, and some of the transcripts can be accessed at the following website: http://etext.virginia.edu/salem/witchcraft/texts/transcripts.html (accessed June 4, 2007).

"more like to be bewitched than she was a witch": Karlsen, *Shape of a Woman*, 36, and Starkey, *Massachusetts*, 42.

sometimes in the form of a beast such as a hog or a "great dog": Van Der Linde, *Salem Village*, 40–42. See this same source for more of Tituba's testimony.

fifty-five of those accused of witchcraft would confess: Hill, *Delusion*, 199.

"Nay, we must not believe these distracted children": Starkey, *Massachusetts*, 54. Starkey further quotes Martha Cory as saying, "I do not believe that there are witches," which, for the Puritans, was tantamount to heresy. Of the accused witches, Cory is reported to have said: "Well, if they are, I could not blame the devil for making witches of them, for they are idle slothful persons and minded nothing that was good."

warrant for the arrest of Martha Cory: Paul Boyer and Stephen Nissenbaum, eds., *Verbatim Transcriptions of the Court Records*, vol. 1, 12. The warrant reads: "Salem, March the 19'th 1691/2 There being Complaint this day made before us, By Edward putnam and Henery Keney Yeoman both of Salem Village, Against Martha Cory the wife of Giles Cory of Salem farmes for suspition of haveing Comitted sundry acts of Witchcraft and thereby donne much hurt and injury unto the Bodys of Ann Putnam the wife of Thomas Putnam of Salem Village Yeoman And Anna Puttnam the daugtter of s'd Thomas putnam and Marcy Lewis Single woman Liveing in s'd

Putnams famyly; also abigail Williams one of mr parries is family and Elizabeth Hubert Doctor Grigs his maid. You are therefore in theire Majest's names hereby required to apprehend and bring; before us. Martha Cory the wife of Giles Cory abovesaid on Munday next being the 21't day of this Instant month, at the house of Lt Nathaniell Ingersalls of Salem Village aboute twelve of the Clock in the day in order to her Examination Relateing to the premises and hereof you are not to faile." (It is signed by Jonathan Corwin, John Hathorne, and Jonathan Corwin.) Essex County Archives, Salem: *Witchcraft*, vol. 1.

"had a Snake that used to Suck": Norton, *Devil's Snare*, 64. The quotes Norton includes in her book are from Deodat Lawson's *Brief and True Narrative*, an account of the witch trials.

"The sheriff came to his house and seized all the goods": Hill, *Delusion*, 172.

Phips appointed nine magistrates to be judges: Hoffer, *Salem Witch Trials*, 86. Trials for capital offenses used juries, but other sorts of trials did not. Defense lawyers were banned in Massachusetts, and it was left to the judges to do the job of defending the accused. For more about the legal procedures in the colonies, see Friedman, *Crime and Punishment*, 18–21.

"A preternatural excrescence of flesh": Hill, *Delusion*, 160

"I am innocent to a witch" and "How do you know then": Hoffer, *Salem Witch Trials*, 91. Bishop was the only person to be convicted based on material evidence—workmen testified to having seen poppets (witch dolls, similar to voodoo dolls) when they were fixing up her house.

that came to be known as Gallows Hill: Hill, *Delusion*, 169. Later, an observer of the hangings would be recorded as having looked out her window to see "those unhappy people hanging on Gallows Hills who were executed for witches by the delusion of the times."

"exceeding tenderness" and "speedy and vigorous prosecution": Ibid., 164, and Hoffer, *Salem Witch Trials*, 63.

Chief Justice William Stoughton urged the members of the jury: Boyer and Nissenbaum, *Salem Possessed*, 7.

"I saw Goody Bibber pull pins": Starkey, *Massachusetts*, 159.

Thirty-nine people had signed a petition: Johnson and Johnson, *Understanding*, 102.

"If they were let alone": Norton, *Devil's Snare*, 71.

"I am no more a witch than you are a wizard": Ibid., 230.

Noyes would suffer an internal hemorrhage: Ibid., 230, 312.

"into an angel of light": Hill, *Delusion*, 179.

"rather chose to undergo what death": Norton, *Devil's Snare*, 278, citing Calef (see bibliography) as her source.

"More weight, more weight": Norton, *Devil's Snare*, 277–78, and Roach, *In the Days*, 296–97.

"loud cries and clamours" and "The Devil has taken upon him": Phips's letters to London are reproduced in George Lincoln Burr, ed., *Narratives of the Witchcraft Cases, 1648–1706* (New York: Barnes & Noble, 1968), 197, and Starkey, *Massachusetts*, 230.

One day the afflicted girls went to investigate: Van Der Linde, *Salem Village*, 61.

"To take away the life of anyone": Hoffer, *Salem Witch Trials*, 196. In his account of the story of the Salem witch trials from a legal perspective, Hoffer says that *Cases of Conscience* is "one of the great works of American legal literature" (130). In it, Mather argues that the worse the crime, the more caution the accusations required.

Sarah Ingersoll, the innkeeper of the tavern: Hill, *Delusion*, 138.

"It was all false": Aronson, *Witchhunt*, 183.

On January 15, 1697: Hoffer, *Salem Witch Trials*, 2, and Starkey, *Massachusetts*, 273–74.

"Such was the darkness of that day": Durst Johnson and Johnson, *Understanding*, 111.

eventually became governor of Massachusetts: Roach, *In the Days*, 373. Starkey, *Massachusetts*, 236, writes that Stoughton was reported to have said, "We were in a way to have cleared the land."

"be humbled before god": Hill, *Delusion*, 215, and Starkey, *Massachusetts*, 269–72.

CHAPTER 2: THE HAYMARKET BOMB TRIAL

"a wild-eyed fiend, armed with a smoking gun and a bomb": Henry David, *The History of the Haymarket Affair: A Study in the American Social-Revolutionary and Labor Movements* (New York: Russell & Russell, 1936), 528.

"These aliens, driven out of Germany and Bohemia": *Chicago Tribune,* May 8, 1886.

"The city went insane": Mary Harris Jones, *The Autobiography of Mother Jones* (1925; repr., Chicago: C. H. Kerr, 1974), 21.

"wild-eyed fiend, armed with a smoking revolver and a bomb": David, *History,* 528.

six heads of states were killed: Barbara Tuchman, *The Proud Tower: A Portrait of the World Before the War, 1890–1914* (New York: Bantam Books, 1967), 72. The six assassinated by anarchists were President Carnot of France in 1894, Premier Canovas of Spain in 1897, Empress Elizabeth of Austria in 1898, King Humbert of Italy in 1900, President McKinley of the United States in 1901, and Premier Canalejas of Spain in 1912.

Dynamite had been invented only in 1867: James Joll, *The Anarchists* (Cambridge: Harvard University Press, 1979), 112–19.

sleeping in alleys and under bridges: James Green, *Death in the Haymarket: A Story of Chicago, the First Labor Movement and the Bombing That Divided Gilded Age America* (New York: Pantheon Books, 2006), 37, and Donald L. Miller, *City of the Century: The Epic of Chicago and the Making of America* (New York: Simon & Schuster, 1997), 135.

it often fell on children to supplement the family income: Miller, *City of the Century,* 223, 458.

Employers shared lists ("blacklists"): David, *History,* 22–23, 42–50.

the most radical city in the United States: Miller, *City of the Century,* 468.

It came as no surprise to workers: Green, *Death in the Haymarket,* 28–33.

a total of thirty men were killed: Ibid., 77–80, and Miller, *City of the Century,* 232–33.

Nowhere was this bitter conviction: Green, *Death in the Haymarket,* 127.

August Spies had come to the United States: Paul Avrich, *The Haymarket Tragedy* (Princeton, NJ: Princeton University Press, 1984), 121–23, and Green, *Death in the Haymarket*, 60–62.

Parsons embraced the cause of black emancipation: Avrich, *Haymarket Tragedy*, 3–25, and Green, *Death in the Haymarket*, 55–58.

Bonfield had told his men to fire: Green, *Death in the Haymarket*, 114–17.

killing as many as four workers: David Roediger and Franklin Rosemont, eds., *Haymarket Scrapbook* (Chicago: Charles H. Kerr, 1986), 14. Historians disagree on the actual number of strikers killed or fatally wounded at the McCormick plant on May 3. The lowest figure is one, the highest four.

"Workingmen, to Arms!!!": Green, *Death in the Haymarket*, 171, and Avrich, *Haymarket Tragedy*, 192–93.

"Attention Workingmen!": David, *History*, 194.

"infamous liar" "Hang him!" "There will be a time": Avrich, *Haymarket Tragedy*, 200.

"Arm yourselves": Ibid., 202–3.

"I want the people to know their mayor is here" and "a violent political harangue against capital": Ibid., 200.

A little before the end of Parsons's speech: Ibid., 204.

Fielden was an immigrant from England: Green, *Death in the Haymarket*, 135.

"A million men hold all the property" and "You have nothing more to do with the law": Avrich, *Haymarket Tragedy*, 205.

Bonfield responded by assembling his men: Ibid.

As they surged forward, the crowd retreated: Green, *Death in the Haymarket*, 6.

"I command you" and "But we are peaceable": Avrich, *Haymarket Tragedy*, 206.

"something like a miniature rocket": Green, *Death in the Haymarket*, 6.

"the anarchists and rioters poured a shower": Ibid.

"Goaded by madness": Ibid., 188–89.

"History is on the move": Ibid., 145.

Newspapers around the nation fanned the fury: David, *History*, 214. David does a thorough job of quoting nationwide sources for their take on the Haymarket incident.

"The city went insane": Jones, *Autobiography*, 21.

"It was my policy to quiet matters down": David, *History*, 222–24.

Twenty-two years old, handsome, strong, and fanatical: Green, *Death in the Haymarket*, 141–42.

Lingg had his hands around one detective's throat: Avrich, *Haymarket Tragedy*, 232.

"a piece of bomb, thrown by a person": Ibid., 232–33.

Less than two weeks later, on May 17: Green, *Death in the Haymarket*, 94.

"anarchism should be suppressed:" Ibid., 94.

The accused, most of whom were associated: Ibid.

George Engel, a fifty-year-old wagon maker: Ibid., 139–40.

Oscar Neebe, a former ship's cook: Ibid., 91.

He was never caught: Avrich, *Haymarket Tragedy*, 235, and Green, *Death in the Haymarket*, 206.

"a deliberate conspiracy, the full details of which": David, *History*, 229.

"an almost total sacrifice of business": Green, *Death in the Haymarket*, 210.

Black himself lacked experience as a criminal lawyer: David, *History*, 230–31.

"never expect . . . to be a free man again": Ibid., 237.

After entering a plea of not guilty: Avrich, *Haymarket Tragedy*, 254–59.

"In the light of the fourth of May": David, *History*, 253–54.

Damaging Gilmer's credibility even further: Avrich, *Haymarket Tragedy*, 269–70.

They laid out the bloodstained uniforms: Ibid., 275–76.

"but one step from republicanism to anarchy" and "flock out again like a lot of rats and vermin": David, *History*, 297–98.

newspapers throughout the nation agreed: Ibid., 320.

She was helped by Nina Van Zandt: Green, *Death in the Haymarket,* 243.

The novelist William Dean Howells: Avrich, *Haymarket Tragedy,* 301–2.

The banker Lyman J. Gage: Green, *Death in the Haymarket,* 259.

Attorneys for the Haymarket defendants appealed their case: David, *History,* 347–71, 375–88.

As the date of the executions approached: Avrich, *Haymarket Tragedy,* 347, 353.

While Oglesby was considering their petitions: Ibid., 376–77.

About two hours after Lingg's death: Ibid., 378.

The men then had to utter their last words: Ibid., 391–94.

Judge Gary was praised: Ibid., 402.

the mayor suspended Bonfield and Schaack: Green, *Death in the Haymarket,* 282–83, and Avrich, *Haymarket Tragedy,* 415–16.

Illinois had a new governor: Avrich, *Haymarket Tragedy,* 416–17.

As Darrow recalled later in his autobiography: David, *History,* 489–90.

"If I conclude to pardon these men": Ibid., 490.

"much of the evidence given" and "No greater damage could possibly threaten": Avrich, *Haymarket Tragedy,* 422–23.

Newspapers and prominent public officials accused Atgeld: Ibid., 424–25.

CHAPTER 3: THE SCOPES "MONKEY" TRIAL

"The contest between evolution and Christianity": Lawrence W. Levine, *Defender of the Faith: The Last Decade, 1915–1925* (Cambridge: Harvard University Press, 1987), 339. Levine devotes a chapter of his biography of William Jennings Bryan to the Scopes trial from the perspective of Bryan's involvement in it.

"I think this case will be remembered": L. Sprague de Camp, *The Great Monkey Trial* (New York: Doubleday, 1968), 423–24.

"The business of America is business: John Bartlett, *Bartlett's Familiar Quotations*, 14th ed. (Boston: Little, Brown and Company, 1968), 911.

PREPARE TO MEET THY GOD!: Mary Lee Settle, *The Scopes Trial: The State of Tennessee v. John Scopes* (New York: Franklin Watts, 1972), 56–60. See Settle for more description of the carnival scene in Dayton.

"the most dangerous man in England": Charles Darwin, *The Origin of Species by Means of Natural Selection* (New York: Penguin Classics, 1985), 14.

"sink the human race into a lower grade": John Willis Clark and Thomas McKenny Hughes, *The Life and Letters of the Reverend Adam Sedgwick* (University Press, published 1890: Original from the University of California. Digitalized March 12, 2007), 357.

"When its whole significance dawns on you": George Bernard Shaw, *Back to Methuselah: A Metabiological Pentateuch* (New York: Brentano's, 1921), xlvi, and George E. Webb, *The Evolution Controversy in America* (Lexington: University Press of Kentucky, 1994), 16. Webb points out on page 16 that Darwin's hypothesis was variably described as being a "mere theory" or a "monstrous assumption." He quotes theologian Charles Alexander Hodge as saying: "Science, so called, when it comes in conflict with truth, is what man is when he comes in conflict with God." According to Hodge, the answer to the question "What is Darwinism?" was "It is atheism."

a minister named Dr. William Bell Riley: Edward J. Larson, *Summer of the Gods: The Scopes Trial and America's Continuing Debate over Science and Religion* (New York: Basic Books, 1997), 35. To learn more about Fundamentalism, see pages 20, 21, 32, and 35–37 in Larson's book. For more about Bryan and the anti-evolution crusade, see pages 39–59 in Larson's book.

"All the ills from which America suffers": Tom McGowen, *The Great Monkey Trial* (New York: Franklin Watts, 1990), 24. For details about how Bryan attributed the decline of populism to the theory of evolution, see Levine, *Defender*, 268–70.

In order to fight the insidious influence: Larson, *Summer*, 37–43, 229–34, and McGowen, *Great Monkey*, 29–34, 94–96.

"The teaching of this theory of evolution": McGowen, *Great Monkey*, 30–34. McGowen's book also has a short introduction by Stephen Jay Gould that frames the debate between science and religion. See Settle, *Scopes Trial*, 28–32, for more on the passing of the Butler Act.

"to teach any theory that denies": Settle, *Scopes Trial*, 30–31.

"Save our children for God!": Ray Ginger, *Six Days or Forever? Tennessee v. John Thomas Scopes* (Boston: Beacon Press, 1958), 6.

"They've got their nerve to pass the buck": Settle, *Scopes Trial*, 30–31.

"Nobody believes it's going to be an active statute": Larson, *Summer*, 59, quoting Austin Peay, "Message for the Governor, 23 March 1925, in *Journal of the House of Representatives.*

"Probably the law will never be applied": Robert Grant and Joseph Katz, *The Great Trials of the Twenties* (New York: Sarpedon, 1998), 49–59.

"Tennessee Bans the Teaching of Evolution": Settle, *Scopes Trial*, 35.

"We are looking for a Tennessee teacher": Webb, *Evolution Controversy*, 5–11. The ACLU's ad in the *Chattanooga Daily News* read in full: "We are looking for a Tennessee teacher to accept our services in testing this law in the courts. Four lawyers think a friendly test can be arranged without costing a teacher his or her job. Distinguished counsel have volunteered their services. All we need now is a willing client."

Rappelyea's interest in the case [and] "This here boy" and "Well, a few days later": Douglas Linder, "The Scopes Trial: An Introduction," Famous Trials in American History, http://www.law.umkc.edu/faculty/projects/ftrials/scopes/scopes.htm (accessed June 4, 2007).

"Why Dayton of All Places": Irving Stone, *Clarence Darrow for the Defense* (New York: Doubleday, 1989), 430. For more on Dayton's preparations for the trial, see Larson, *Summer*, 139–42.

Scopes agreed to volunteer: John T. Scopes and James Presley, *Center of the Storm: Memoirs of John T. Scopes* (New York: Holt, Rinehart, and Winston, 1967), 56–62. This book also details Scopes's account of his meeting with town officials.

"It was just a drugstore discussion": Ginger, *Six Days*, 20, 45.

"a local affair, a case among friends": Ibid., 45.

"We cannot afford to have a system": Ibid., 21.

"The sin of this generation" and "not more brains but more heart": Levine, *Defender*, 279. Levine uses Bryan's words from his newspaper *The Commoner* in 1921.

"Such a conception of man's origin": Ibid., 261, 262. Quoting Bryan from his famous "Prince of Peace" speech, Levine says that Bryan preferred to believe that "love rather than hatred is the law of development" (261).

Darrow's letter consisted of fifty-five questions: Clarence Darrow, *The Story of My Life* (New York: Charles Scribner's Sons, 1932), 266.

"felt Darrow was a headline chaser" and "would become a carnival": Grant and Katz, *Great Trials*, 150, and Ginger, *Six Days*, 45. In his memoir, Scopes, who developed a lasting friendship with Darrow, also offers some insights into the famous lawyer's character; see Scopes and Presley, *Center of the Storm*, 66–74. See Ginger, *Six Days*, 77–80, and McGowen, *Great Monkey*, 56–60, 64–65, 73–74, for more about the different views among the defense attorneys.

Third, they wanted to address the issue of academic freedom: Larson, *Summer*, 133–45, and McGowen, *Great Monkey*, 48–49. Years after the trial, Darrow writes: "My object, and my only object, was to focus the attention of the country on the programme of Mr. Bryan and the other fundamentalists in America" (Levine, *Defender*, 332–33). Levine quotes Arthur Garfield Hays as saying that the trial "was a battle between two types of mind—the rigid, orthodox, accepting, unyielding, narrow, conventional mind, and the broad liberal, critical, cynical, skeptical and tolerant mind" (133).

they secured tents from the War Department: Ginger, *Six Days*, 73.

Hollywood film studios sent motion-picture cameramen: Settle, *Scopes Trial*, 36, and Scopes and Presley, *Center of the Storm*, 98–100.

WE HANDLE ALL KINDS OF MEAT: Grant and Katz, *Great Trials*, 154.

YOUR OLD MAN'S A MONKEY: Darrow, *Story of My Life*, 258, and Grant and Katz, *Great Trials*, 49–59.

barbecue pit on the lawn: Scopes and Presley, *Center of the Storm*, 94–100. For more on the carnival atmosphere in Dayton during the trial, see Tom Streissguth, *An Eyewitness History: The Roaring Twenties* (New York: Facts on File, 2001), 160–61. The Anti-Evolution League of America was formed in 1924 in order to support challenges to anti-evolution legislation.

"John the Baptist the Third" and "Deck Carter": Scopes and Presley, *Center of the Storm*, 94–100, and Streissguth, *Eyewitness History*, 160–61.

"All sorts of weird cults were present": Darrow, *Story of My Life*, 261–62.

"What is the secret of the world's interest": Levine, *Defender*, 339.

There was no crowd to greet him: Darrow, *Story of My Life*, 251. Darrow writes in his autobiography: "There was no torchlight parade to greet me as I stepped off the train. I did not miss it much, with the thermometer blazing away toward the hundred mark, where it remained nearly all the time that we were there." For more about Bryan's and Darrow's arrivals in Dayton, see Settle, *Scopes Trial*, 61–65, and Don Nardo, *The Scopes Trial* (San Diego: Lucent Books, 1997), 37.

Dayton's courtroom was quite grand: Settle, *Scopes Trial*, 67.

"blast furnace": *H. L. Mencken on Religion*, edited by S. T. Joshi (Amherst, NY: Prometheus Books, 2002), 178.

Later, the sheriff would install ceiling fans: Scopes and Presley, *Center of the Storm*, 143–49, and Darrow, *Story of My Life*, 256. Darrow writes further of the terrible heat: "Tennessee must be very close to the equator; or maybe the crust is very thin under this little sin-fearing section, or, where could such hellish heat come from."

No woman had ever served on a jury: Ginger, *Six Days*, 71, and de Camp, *Great Monkey*, 118.

"When I was a boy": Settle, *Scopes Trial*, 59–60, and Ginger, *Six Days*, 73.

Neal charged that the Butler law violated: McGowen, *Great Monkey*, 56–57.

Underscoring just how unreasonable he found the Butler statute to be: Larson, *Summer*, 159.

Dudley Malone followed by stating: Scopes and Presley, *Center of the Storm*, 110–11. See this same source for more of an overview summary of the opening arguments.

"as if it were a death struggle" and "Here we find today": Scopes and Presley, *Center of the Storm*, 111–17.

"This case is a conflict between science and religion": Stone, *Clarence Darrow*, 443.

"whether or not a schoolteacher has taught" and "the agnostic counsel for the Defense": Grant and Katz, *Great Trials*, 159.

"All we have to do is get to the fact": Ginger, *Six Days*, 112, and Grant and Katz, *Great Trials*, 159.

the high point of which was the testimony of two high school boys: Sadakat Kadri, *The Trial: A History, from Socrates to O. J. Simpson* (New York: Random House, 2005), 280–81.

"You didn't leave the church when he told you": Scopes and Presley, *Center of the Storm*, 132–34.

"Every single word that was said against this defendant": Larson, *Summer*, 446.

"denies the story of the Divine Creation": Settle, *Scopes Trial*, 30–31. (For more on the debate about scientific testimony, see pages 86–94 in Settle's book and Larson, *Summer*, 173–75.)

"the change of one organism from one character" and "As far as I'm concerned, they can teach": Settle, *Scopes Trial*, 84–85.

"We expect to show": Ibid., 86.

"pseudoscientific" material to be interjected [and] "The people of this state": Scopes and Presley, *Center of the Storm*, 143–49. Ginger, *Six Days*, quotes Bryan as writing, "If we can shut out the expert testimony, which is intended to prevent the enforcement of the law by proving that it ought not to have been passed—a perfectly absurd proposition—we will be through in a short time" (80).

"Mr. Bryan, Your Honor, is not" and "Keep it as your consolation": Scopes and Presley, *Center of the Storm*, 151–54.

"reading the tragedy on his beaten face": Ibid., 147–56. Scopes says in his memoir: "I have never seen such a great change hit a human being as fast as it did Bryan. Malone spoke for not more than twenty minutes. There was only dejection on Bryan's face; the victory that had been his only a few moments before was suddenly, disastrously dissipated." For more about Malone's speech and its effect on Bryan, see Levine, *Defender*, 346.

"I do not understand why every request": Ginger, *Six Days*, 141–50.

visitors bundled their chairs and their families: Ibid., 153.

there didn't seem much point to spending any more time: Ibid.

"Do you think the earth was made" through "I am simply trying to protect the word of God": Kadri, *The Trial*, 283, and Scopes and Presley, *Center of the Storm*, 164–83.

For more on Darrow's famous questioning of Bryan, see Ginger, *Six Days*, 168–74. Darrow writes in his autobiography (*Story of My Life*, 267): "When court adjourned it became evident that the audience had been thinking, and perhaps felt that they had heard something worth while. Much to my surprise, the great gathering began to surge toward me. They seemed to have changed sides in a single afternoon. A friendly crowd followed me toward my home. Mr. Bryan left the grounds practically alone."

not what role God had to play: de Camp, *Great Monkey*, 417.

William Jennings Bryan stayed in Dayton: Levine, *Defender*, 356.

"We see nothing to be gained by prolonging": Webb, *Evolution Controversy*, 5–11.

"Within twelve months, every state in the Union": de Camp, *Great Monkey*, 459.

only two states passed anti-evolution legislation: Samuel Walker, *In Defense of American Liberties* (New York: Oxford University Press, 1990), 75, and de Camp, *Great Monkey*, 459.

Some publishers—including the publisher of the book: de Camp, *Great Monkey*, 457, and Walker, *In Defense*, 76. Textbook publishers Holt, Macmillan, and Allyn & Bacon all rolled out nonevolution editions of their science books.

"I'm a Christian mother who believes" and high school superintendent held a public bonfire: de Camp, *Great Monkey*, 457, 459.

CHAPTER FOUR: THE TRIALS OF ALGER HISS

"Mr. Hiss represents the concealed enemy": Sam Tanenhaus, *Whittaker Chambers: A Biography* (New York: Random House, 1997), 274.

"Getting the facts about Whittaker Chambers": John Cabot Smith, *Alger Hiss: The True Story* (New York: Penguin, 1977), 231, and Allen Weinstein, *Perjury: The Hiss-Chambers Case* (New York: Random House, 1997), 44.

for a hearing of the House Un-American Activities Committee: Walter Goodman, *The Committee* (New York: Farrar, Straus and Giroux, 1968). This book provides an excellent history of HUAC. See Smith, *Alger Hiss*, 232–33, for the appearance of the hearing room and the presence of television sets. According to Smith, Richard Nixon, who led HUAC's investigation of Alger Hiss, said that he wished more people had television sets.

a shocking accusation against Alger Hiss: Weinstein, *Perjury*, 3–69. This book tells the story of HUAC's investigation leading to the August 25 hearing.

"The story has spread that in testifying": Tanenhaus, *Whittaker Chambers*, 274. For a video clip of Chambers's speech, see Whittaker Chambers, "Chambers' Higher Purpose," The Alger Hiss Story, http://homepages.nyu.edu/~th15 (accessed July 9, 2007). This pro-Hiss website, based on the work of Alger Hiss's friend and lawyer, John Lowenthal, is a good introduction to the world of the conspiracy theory as related to the Hiss case.

The war's end had left the Soviet Union's Red Army: Martin Walker, *The Cold War: A History* (New York: Henry Holt, 1995), 10–57. See this source for more on Russia's postwar expansion; see also Michael McGwire, "National Security and Soviet Foreign Policy," in *Origins of the Cold War: An International History*, ed. Melvyn P. Leffler and David S. Painter (London: Routledge, 1994), 63–71.

could weaken the United States in its international conflict: Ellen Schrecker, *Many Are the Crimes: McCarthyism in America* (New York: Little, Brown, 1998). This book tells the story of the anti-Communist movement in America before and after the red-baiting career of Senator Joseph McCarthy.

According to his 1952 autobiography, *Witness*: Whittaker Chambers, *Witness* (New York: Random House, 1952), 191. This book tells the story of Chambers's career, and it is valuable for anyone who wishes to experience the mood of the cold war at its most intense and especially the feeling of people of conscience that the times were forcing them to make terrible choices. *Witness* is also a memoir of the American Communist Party in the 1920s and 1930s, and Chambers describes individual members with considerable sympathy in their human variety.

Chambers worked for Soviet spy networks: Tanenhaus, *Whittaker Chambers*, 79–119. This book tells the story of Chambers's career as a Soviet spy.

Chambers had recently received one of these alarming invitations: Weinstein, *Perjury*, 310–12. This source details Chambers's summons to Moscow and why he had good reason to consider it dangerous. Under Stalin's direction in the 1930s, the Soviets were "purging" (getting rid of) many citizens of the Soviet Union, and they were doing the same thing in their spy networks.

this was just what he intended to do: Chambers, *Witness*, 453.

He named several people as secret Communist Party members: Tanenhaus, *Whittaker Chambers*, 161–62.

and a fierce critic of the Soviet Union: Weinstein, *Perjury*, 342–45.

Chambers began testifying before HUAC: Ibid., 5, and Chambers, *Witness*, 538.

"Hell, why is this in executive session?": Weinstein, *Perjury*, 5.

"he absolutely refused to break" and "I was very fond of Mr. Hiss": Alistair Cooke, *A Generation on Trial: U.S.A. v. Alger Hiss* (New York: Alfred A. Knopf, 1952), 58.

the most influential and admired men and women: Weinstein, *Perjury*, 11, 43, 72–81, 361–63, 376. See this source for more details of Hiss's career and the trust placed in him.

According to the American mind, a Communist was an unnatural person: Victor S. Navasky, *Naming Names* (New York: Viking Press, 1980), 15–16. The description of the "typical Communist" as imagined by the American mind early in the cold war is based on "Cold War Cinema II" by Nora Sayre, published in *The Nation*, March 3, 1979, quoted in Navasky's book. His book is an absorbing account of McCarthyism in Hollywood.

"I am not and never have been a member" and "laid eyes on": Weinstein, *Perjury*, 10.

"We've been had! We're ruined": Ibid., 11–15.

"This case is going to kill the Committee": Ibid., 11.

"Let's wash our hands of the whole mess": Ibid.

Nixon was made head of a subcommittee: Ibid., 16–17.

It was possible that Crosley and Chambers: Smith, *Alger Hiss*, 183–98, and Weinstein, *Perjury*, 21–34.

"Mr. Hiss, the man standing here is Mr. Whittaker Chambers": Alger Hiss, *In the Court of Public Opinion* (New York: Alfred A. Knopf, 1957), 85; Chambers, *Witness*, 603.

"perspiring and very pale" and "would not meet [his] eye": Hiss, *Court of Public Opinion*, 85.

"I was swept by a sense of pity": Chambers, *Witness*, 603.

the man he and his wife had known as George Crosley: Ibid., 607, and Smith, *Alger Hiss*, 219–24.

"to discredit recent great achievements" and "Is he a man of consistent reliability": Smith, *Alger Hiss*, 231, and Weinstein, *Perjury*, 44.

where he would not be immune to being sued for libel: Cooke, *Generation*, 85–91, and Weinstein, *Perjury*, 44–51. Both sources provide a description of the famous August 25 hearing in which Chambers and Hiss testified before HUAC.

"80 percent at least fabrication": Weinstein, *Perjury*, 44–51.

on the radio program *Meet the Press*: Tanenhaus, *Whittaker Chambers*, 275–78.

Alger Hiss demanded that Whittaker Chambers pay him: Chambers, *Witness*, 722. A few days later, Hiss upped the amount he was suing for to $75,000.

"I welcome Mr. Hiss's daring suit": Tanenhaus, *Whittaker Chambers*, 283.

In the novel, *Class Reunion*, two former classmates: Weinstein, *Perjury*, 179–84. Weinstein further describes the investigation in his book.

saw homosexuality as a symptom of mental illness: Tanenhaus, *Whittaker Chambers*, 343–45. Tanenhaus also details the FBI interviews in which Chambers testifies to his homosexual experiences, or, as Chambers puts it, "certain facts which should be told only to a priest."

"I thought I had destroyed them: Weinstein, *Perjury*, 165.

Hiss had taken the originals back to the office: Ibid., 169–79.

the newspapers dubbed this new batch of evidence: Ibid., 185–93.

The typewriter was finally located: Ibid., 301–2, 304–5, 386–91, 406.

But if the typewriter had not been in the possession: Ibid., 386–97.

"a moral leper": "A Well-Lighted Arena," *Time*, June 13, 1949. This article is available on the web at www.time.com/time/magazine/article/0,9171,800284-1,00.html.

The law required a unanimous decision: Weinstein, *Perjury*, 437–49.

I would like to thank your Honor": Cooke, *Generation*, 338.

In the imagination of angry Republicans: Weinstein, *Perjury,* 510. Weinstein further explains: "To hear [some Republicans] tell it . . . Hiss practically lived at FDR's side during the Crimean conference."

Republican senator Joseph McCarthy of Wisconsin: Richard H. Rover, *Senator Joe McCarthy* (New York: Harcourt, Brace & World, 1959), 125.

"here in [his] hand": "Enemies from Within: Senator Joseph R. McCarthy's Accusations of Disloyalty," available at http://historymatters.gmu.edu/d/6456. This site gives the text of McCarthy's Wheeling speech.

"loyalty" and "one as to his judgment": Weinstein, *Perjury,* 511.

"Then we got the evidence" and ALGER HISS SEES 4 WORDS: *New York Times,* May 3, 1974.

Alger Hiss officially requested that the 1950 verdict: Weinstein, *Perjury,* 503.

"Not a single document" and "I was not properly understood": Ibid., 504–5.

"His attorney, Lowenthal, pushed me": March Richer, "The Ongoing Campaign of Alger Hiss: the Sins of the Father," *Modern Age,* Fall 2004.

Other evidence released in the 1990s: Allen Weinstein and Alexander Vassiliev, *The Haunted Wood: Soviet Espionage in America—the Stalin Era* (New York: Random House, 1999), 5–8. Other documentary evidence of Hiss's guilt released in the 1990s is discussed in Weinstein, *Perjury,* 507–13. When Alger Hiss died, many news agencies and newspaper and television commentators were under the impression that he had been exonerated by the release of Soviet archives, adding to the mythology that continues to surround the case: Weinstein, *Perjury,* 506.

CHAPTER 5: THE TRIALS OF ZACARIAS MOUSSAOUI

"After all we are in AMERICA": Daniel Pipes, "Zacarias Moussaoui Asked, Can an Airplane Pilot Shut off Oxygen to Passengers?" Frontpagemagazine.com, April 29, 2005.

"Hello, Mrs. Matt, I am Mrs. Zacarias": Jim Yardley, "E-Mail Sent to Flight School Gave Terror Suspect's 'Goal,'" *New York Times,* February 8, 2002, East Coast edition.

"But I am sure that you can do something": Pipes, "Zacarias Moussaoui Asked."

He arrived in Eagan in early August of 2001: Ibid.

"an ego trip": Ibid.

"I am nothing": Phil Hirschkorn, "Moussaoui Was a Flight School Washout," CNN.com, March 9, 2006, www.cnn.com/2006/LAW/03/09/moussaoui.trial/ (accessed June 4, 2007).

"just a weird duck": Pipes, "Zacarias Moussaoui Asked."

"I'm calling on a customer": Ibid.

FBI agent Harry Samit arrested Moussaoui: Neil A. Lewis, "Agent Says He Thought Moussaoui Knew About Plot," *New York Times*, March 10, 2006, East Coast edition.

a 747, with all its jet fuel, would make a powerful bomb: Philip Shenon, "Flight School Warned F.B.I. of Suspicions," *New York Times*, December 22, 2001, East Coast edition.

It is possible that this warrant might have been granted: Romesh Ratnesar and Michael Weisskopf, "How the FBI Blew the Case," *Time*, June 3, 2002.

"If the application for a FISA warrant": Letter from Sen. Grassley to FBI Director Mueller Re FISA, 1/9/2003. www.techlawjournal.com/cong108/fisa/20030109.asp.

But the official failed to act on the information: Neil A. Lewis, "F.B.I. Agent Testifies Superiors Didn't Pursue Moussaoui Case," *New York Times*, March 21, 2006, East Coast edition.

resulting in the deaths of everyone on board: National Commission on Terrorist Attacks upon the United States, "We Have Some Planes," in *The 9/11 Commission Report: Final Report of the National Commission on Terrorists Attacks upon the United States* (Washington, DC: U.S. Government Printing Office, 2004), 1–34.

considered any action taken against it to be justified: National Commission on Terrorist Attacks upon the United States, "The Foundation of the New Terrorism," in *9/11 Commission Report*, 47–54.

So, too, had Moussaoui: Viveca Novak, "How the Moussaoui Case Crumbled," *Time*, October 27, 2003.

The knives found among Moussaoui's belongings: This information is found in the government's indictment against Moussaoui, *United States of America v. Zacarias Moussaoui, a/k/a "Shaqil" a/k/a "Abu Khalid al Sahrawi," defendant.*

www.usdoj.gov/ag/moussaouiindictment.htm. The indictment also appears with the title *US v. Zacarias Moussaoui* in news.findlaw.com/hdocs/docs/moussaoui/usmouss 71602spind.pdf.

"an al-Qaeda mistake and a missed opportunity": "The System Was Blinking Red," in *9/11 Commission Report,* 273.

"How could he be involved": Suzanne Daley, "Mysterious Life of a Suspect from France," *New York Times,* September 21, 2001, East Coast edition.

"a likeable boy, tenacious, a slow worker": Ibid.

a serious psychiatric disorder from which Moussaoui: Susan Dominus, "Everybody Has a Mother," *New York Times Magazine,* February 23, 2003.

"She told them that they were not acting like men": Suzanne Daley, "Mysterious Life."

This money probably helped him pay: Ibid.

a civilian court or by military tribunal: Don Van Natta Jr., "Debate Centers on Which Court Will Decide Fate of Arab Man," *New York Times,* November 22, 2001, East Coast edition.

President George W. Bush had signed an executive order: Office of the Press Secretary, "President Issues Military Order: Detention, Treatment, and Trial of Certain Non-Citizens in the War Against Terrorism," U.S. Government Press Release, November 13, 2001.

"the legal equivalent of outer space": John Barry, Michael Hirsh, and Michael Isakoff, "The Roots of Torture," *Newsweek International;* available at www.nsnbc .msn.com/id/4989481/ (accessed June 4, 2007).

The treatment of the prisoners at Guantánamo Bay: Ibid.

"conspiring with Osama bin Laden and Al Qaeda": *United States of America v. Zacarias Moussaoui, a/k/a "Shaqil" a/k/a "Abu Khalid al Sahrawi," defendant.*

Specifically, Moussaoui was charged with conspiracy: Ibid.

where jurors tended to favor the death penalty: Don Van Natta, Jr., with Benjamin Weiser, "Compromise Settles Debate over Tribunal," *New York Times*, December 12, 2001, East Coast edition.

She belonged in a judicial "hall of shame": Philip Shenon and Neil A. Lewis, "Unpredictable Judge for Terrorism Suspect," *New York Times*, December 26, 2001, East Coast edition.

All three were morally and professionally committed: Philip Shenon with Benjamin Weiser, "2 Rival Legal Teams for '20th Hijacker' Case," *New York Times*, December 18, 2001, East Coast edition.

informally known as the "rocket docket": Philip Shenon, "U.S. Sees Threat to Terror Trial," *New York Times*, October 23, 2002, East Coast edition.

"In the name of Allah, I do not have anything to plead": David Johnston, "Not-Guilty Plea Is Set for Man in Terror Case," *New York Times*, January 3, 2002, East Coast edition.

the trial, set to begin in the fall of that year: Ibid.

"the destruction of the United States" through "innocent until proven guilty": Novak, "How the Moussaoui Case Crumbled."

"You're obviously a very smart man": Philip Shenon, "Terror Suspect Says He Wants U.S. Destroyed," *New York Times*, April 23, 2002, East Coast edition.

he would "not participate in an obscene Jewish science": Philip Shenon, "In Motions, Defendant Declares He Is Hostile to Jews and U.S.," *New York Times*, June 18, 2002, East Coast edition.

he agreed to submit to a two-hour psychiatric examination: Philip Shenon, "Defendant Yields on Refusal to See Psychiatrist," *New York Times*, May 31, 2002, East Coast edition, and Philip Shenon, "Court Psychiatrist Concludes Defendant Is Not Mentally Ill," *New York Times*, June 8, 2002, East Coast edition.

Brinkema found them unconvincing: Neil A. Lewis, "Mental Issue Keeps Grip on Sept. 11 Case," *New York Times*, July 10, 2002, East Coast edition, and Eric Lichtblau, "Judge Rules 9/11 Defendant Is Competent to Plead Guilty," *New York Times*, April 21, 2005, East Coast edition.

"frivolous, scandalous, disrespectful or repetitive" court papers: Philip Shenon, "Judge Bars 9/11 Suspect from Being Own Lawyer," *New York Times*, November 15, 2003, East Coast edition.

Moussaoui was entitled to interview: Philip Shenon, "Man Charged in Sept. 11 Attacks Demands That Qaeda Leaders Testify," *New York Times*, March 22, 2003, East Coast edition.

ordered that he be permitted to submit written questions: Philip Shenon, "Government Lawyers Fear 9/11 Ruling Threatens Qaeda Cases," *New York Times*, October 4, 2003, East Coast edition.

in effect upholding the decision: Linda Greenhouse, "Justices Refuse to Consider Law Banning Gay Adoption," *New York Times*, January 11, 2005, East Coast edition, and Linda Greenhouse, "After 5 Months' Absence, Rehnquist Is Back in Court," *New York Times*, March 22, 2005, East Coast edition.

"I came to the United States" and "I am guilty of a broad conspiracy": Neil A. Lewis, "Moussaoui Tells Court He's Guilty of a Terror Plot," *New York Times*, April 23, 2005, East Coast edition.

that was enough for him to have been responsible: Neil A. Lewis, "Jury in Virginia Will Decide Life or Death for Moussaoui," *New York Times*, February 6, 2006, East Coast edition.

They faced "an awesome responsibility": Neil A. Lewis, "Moussaoui Ejected Four Times for Disrupting Jury Selection," *New York Times*, February 7, 2006, East Coast edition.

"I won't be heard by this court": Ibid.

he shouted, "God curse America": Neil A. Lewis, "Judge Ejects 9/11 Suspect After Outburst," *New York Times*, February 15, 2006, East Coast edition.

the jury pool was gradually whittled down: Neil A. Lewis, "Moussaoui Ejected Four Times," and Neil A. Lewis, "Defendant in 9/11 Case Heeds Judge," *New York Times*, February 16, 2006, East Coast edition.

but were inwardly compelled to watch: Neil A. Lewis, "At Satellite Courthouses, 9/11 Relatives Will Watch Moussaoui's Sentencing," *New York Times*, March 5, 2006, East Coast edition.

the four-hour videotape included Moussaoui's cross-examination: Neil A. Lewis, "Prosecutors Show Tape at Sept. 11 Trial," *New York Times*, March 9, 2006, East Coast edition.

Then the prosecution put on Moussaoui's flight instructor: Neil A. Lewis, "Agent Says He Thought Moussaoui Knew About Plot," *New York Times*, March 10, 2006, East Coast edition.

"In all my years on the bench": Jerry Markon and Timothy Dwyer, "Judge Halts Terror Trial; Lawyer E-Mailed Court Transcripts to 7 Witnesses," *Washington Post*, March 14, 2006, and Neil A. Lewis, "Judge Calls Halt to Penalty Phase of Terror Trial," *New York Times*, March 14, 2006, East Coast edition.

the judge instead disqualified the aviation officials: Neil A. Lewis, "Judge Penalizes Moussaoui Prosecutors by Barring Major Witnesses," *New York Times*, March 15, 2006, East Coast edition.

they still wouldn't have been able to act quickly enough: Neil A. Lewis, "F.B.I. Agent Testifies Superiors Didn't Pursue Moussaoui Case."

The prosecution rested after these witnesses: Neil A. Lewis, "Case for Moussaoui Execution Seems Bolstered by 2 Witnesses," *New York Times*, March 23, 2006, East Coast edition, and Neil A. Lewis and David Johnston, "Focus on F.B.I.'s 9/11 Signals," *New York Times*, March 25, 2006, East Coast edition.

He said he had known of the 9/11 plot: Neil A. Lewis, "Moussaoui, Undermining Case, Now Ties Himself to 9/11 Plot," *New York Times*, March 28, 2006, East Coast edition.

"not right in the head and having a bad character": Neil A. Lewis, "Defense Tries to Undo Damage Moussaoui Did," *New York Times*, March 29, 2006, East Coast edition. This article also describes the testimony of Thomas J. Pickard.

"I don't know, with all the information the FBI collects": Neil A. Lewis and Scott Shane, "Defense Tries to Undo Damage Moussaoui Did," *New York Times*, March 29, 2006, East Coast edition.

"Zacarias Moussaoui came to this country to kill" through "Show him we are not the hate-filled vengeful Americans": Neil A. Lewis, "Moussaoui Sentencing Case Goes to the Jury," *New York Times*, March 30, 2006, East Coast edition. This article encapsulates and quotes from the summations of the prosecution and the defense.

"You'll never get my blood!": Neil A. Lewis, "Jurors Permit Death Penalty for Moussaoui," *New York Times*, April 4, 2006, East Coast edition.

would surely give far greater weight to the aggravating factors: Neil A. Lewis, "Jury in Virginia Will Decide Life or Death for Moussaoui."

"That image comes back to haunt me every day": Neil A. Lewis and Scott Shane, "Defense Tries to Undo Damage Moussaoui Did," *New York Times*, March 29, 2006, East Coast edition.

A man from India told of his sister's suicide: Neil A. Lewis, "Moussaoui Jury Hears of Impact and Grief," *New York Times*, April 7, 2006, East Coast edition.

His mother had often been beaten badly enough: Neil A. Lewis, "Moussaoui's Childhood Is Presented as Mitigating Factor," *New York Times*, April 18, 2006, East Coast edition.

he had displayed classic schizophrenic symptoms: Neil A. Lewis, "Witness Says Moussaoui Exhibited Mental Illness," *New York Times*, April 19, 2006, East Coast edition.

the jury knew these witnesses were testifying for the defense: Neil A. Lewis, "Jury Hears 9/11 Relatives Against Killing Moussaoui," *New York Times*, April 20, 2006, East Coast edition.

"America you lost, I won!": Jerry Markon and Timothy Dwyer, "Jurors Reject Death Penalty for Moussaoui, *Washington Post*, May 4, 2006.

they agreed that Moussaoui had been at most a bit player: Neil A. Lewis, "Moussaoui Given Life Term by Jury over Link to 9/11," *New York Times*, May 4, 2006, East Coast edition.

Bibliography

THE SALEM WITCH TRIALS

Aronson, Marc. *John Winthrop, Oliver Cromwell and the Land of Promise.* New York: Clarion Books, 2004.

Boyer, Paul, and Stephen Nissenbaum. *Salem Possessed: The Social Origins of Witchcraft.* Cambridge: Harvard University Press, 1976.

————. *The Salem Witchcraft Papers: Verbatim Transcripts of the Legal Documents of the Salem Witchcraft Outbreak of 1692.* New York: Da Capo Press, 1977.

Burr, George Lincoln, ed. *Narratives of the Witchcraft Cases, 1648–1706.* New York: Barnes & Noble, 1968.

Calef, Robert. "More Wonders of the Invisible World; or, The Wonders of the Invisible World Display'd in Five Parts." In *Narratives of the Witchcraft Cases, 1648–1706,* edited by George Lincoln Burr. New York: Barnes & Noble, 1968.

Doherty, Kiernan. *Puritans, Pilgrims, and Merchants: Founders of the Northeastern Colonies.* Minneapolis: Oliver Press, 1999.

Fremon, David K. *The Salem Witchcraft Trials in American History.* Berkeley Heights, NJ: Enslow, 1999.

Friedman, Lawrence M. *Crime and Punishment in American History.* New York: Basic Books, 1993.

Hill, Frances. *A Delusion of Satan: The Full Story of the Salem Witch Trials.* New York: Doubleday, 1995.

————. *Salem Witch Trials Reader.* New York: Da Capo Press, 2000.

Hoffer, Peter Charles. *The Salem Witchcraft Trials: A Legal History.* Lawrence: University Press of Kansas, 1997.

Johnson, Claudia Durst, and Vernon E. Johnson. *Understanding "The Crucible."* Westport, CT: Greenwood Press, 1998.

Kadri, Sadakat. *The Trial: A History, from Socrates to O.J. Simpson.* New York: Random House, 2005.

Kallen, Stuart A. *The Salem Witch Trials.* San Diego: Lucent Books, 1999.

Karlsen, Carol F. *The Devil in the Shape of a Woman.* New York: Vintage Books, 1987.

Knappman, Edward W., Stephen G. Christianson, and Lisa Paddock. *Great American Trials.* San Diego: Gale Research, 1994.

Lawson, Deodat. *A Brief True Narrative of Some Remarkable Passages Relating to Sundry Persons Afflicted by Witchcraft, at Salem Village Which Happened from the Nineteenth of March to the Fifth of April 1692.* Boston, 1692.

Miller, Arthur. *The Crucible.* Philadelphia: Chelsea House Publishers, 1999.

Norton, Mary Beth. *In the Devil's Snare.* New York: Alfred A. Knopf, 2002.

Roach, Marilynne. *In the Days of the Salem Witchcraft Trials.* Boston: Houghton Mifflin, 1996.

Robinson, Enders A. *The Devil Discovered: Salem Witchcraft 1692.* Long Grove, IL: Waveland Press, 2001.

Starkey, Marion L. *The Devil in Massachusetts.* New York: Alfred A. Knopf, 1949.

Van Der Linde, Laurel. *The Devil in Salem Village: The Story of the Salem Witchcraft Trials.* Spotlight on American History. Brookfield, CT: Millbrook Press, 1992.

THE HAYMARKET BOMB TRIAL

Avrich, Paul. *The Haymarket Tragedy.* Princeton, NJ: Princeton University Press, 1984.

Chicago: City of the Century. Film in PBS series The American Experience (www.pbs.org/wgbh/amex/chicago).

David, Henry. *The History of the Haymarket Affair: A Study in the American Social-Revolutionary and Labor Movements.* New York: Russell & Russell, 1936.

Green, James. *Death in the Haymarket: A Story of Chicago, the First Labor Movement, and the Bombing That Divided Gilded Age America.* New York: Pantheon Books, 2006.

Joll, James. *The Anarchists.* Cambridge: Harvard University Press, 1979.

Jones, Mary Harris. *The Autobiography of Mother Jones.* Chicago: C. H. Kerr, 1925.

Miller, Donald L. *City of the Century: The Epic of Chicago and the Making of America.* New York: Simon & Schuster, 1997.

Roediger, David, and Franklin Rosemont, eds. *Haymarket Scrapbook.* Chicago: Charles H. Kerr, 1986.

Tuchman, Barbara. *The Proud Tower: A Portrait of the World Before the War, 1890–1914*. New York: Bantam Books, 1967.

THE SCOPES "MONKEY" TRIAL

Clark, John Willis, and Thomas McKenny Hughes. *The Life and Letters of the Reverend Adam Sedgwick*. University of California, 1890. Original digitalized March 12, 2007.

Darrow, Clarence. *The Story of My Life*. London: Charles Scribner's Sons, 1932.

Darwin, Charles. *The Origin of Species by Means of Natural Selection*. New York: Penguin Classics, 1985.

De Camp, Sprague L. *The Great Monkey Trial*. New York: Doubleday, 1968.

Kadri, Sadakat. *The Trial: A History, from Socrates to O.J. Simpson*. New York: Random House, 2005.

Ginger, Ray. *Six Days or Forever? Tennessee v. John Thomas Scopes*. Boston: Beacon Press, 1958.

Grant, Robert, and Joseph Katz. *The Great Trials of the Twenties*. Rockville Center, NY: Sarpedon, 1998.

Hanson, Freya Ottem. *The Scopes Monkey Trial*. Berkeley Heights, NJ: Enslow, 2000.

Hellman, Hal. *Great Feuds in Science*. New York: John Wiley and Sons, 1998.

Kallen, Stuart. *The Roaring Twenties*. San Diego: Lucent Books, 2002.

Karp, Walter. *Charles Darwin and the Origin of Species*. London: Cassell, 1968.

Larson, Edward J. *Summer of the Gods: The Scopes Trial and America's Continuing Debate over Science and Religion*. New York: Basic Books, 1997.

Levine, Lawrence W. *Defender of the Faith: The Last Decade, 1915–1925*. Cambridge: Harvard University Press, 1987.

McGowen, Tom. *The Great Monkey Trial*. New York: Franklin Watts, 1990.

Nardo, Don. *The Scopes Trial*. San Diego: Lucent Books, 1997.

Numbers, Ronald L. *The Creationists: The Evolution of Scientific Creationism*. New York: Alfred A. Knopf, 1992.

Pietrusza, David. *The Roaring Twenties: World History Series*. San Diego: Lucent Books, 1998.

Scopes, John T., and James Presley. *Center of the Storm: Memoirs of John T. Scopes.* New York: Holt, Rinehart, and Winston, 1967.

Settle, Mary Lee. *The Scopes Trial: The State of Tennessee v. John Scopes.* New York: Franklin Watts, 1972.

Shaw, George Bernard. *Back to Methuselah: A Metabiological Pentateuch.* New York: Brentano's, 1921.

Sonder, Ben. *Evolutionism and Creationism.* New York: Franklin Watts, 1999.

Stone, Irving. *Clarence Darrow for the Defense.* New York: Doubleday, 1989.

Streissguth, Tom. *An Eyewitness History: The Roaring Twenties.* New York: Facts on File, 2001.

Webb, George E. *The Evolution Controversy in America.* Lexington: University Press of Kentucky, 1994.

Weinberg, Arthur and Lila. *Clarence Darrow: A Sentimental Rebel.* New York: Putnam's Sons, 1980.

THE TRIALS OF ALGER HISS

Chambers, Whittaker. *Witness.* New York: Random House, 1952.

Cook, Alistair. *A Generation on Trial: U.S.A. v. Alger Hiss.* New York: Alfred A. Knopf, 1952.

Goodman, Walter. *The Committee.* New York: Farrar, Straus and Giroux, 1968.

Hiss, Alger. *In the Court of Public Opinion.* New York: Alfred A. Knopf, 1957.

Navasky, Victor. *Naming Names.* New York: Viking Press, 1980.

Rover, Richard H. *Senator Joe McCarthy.* New York: Harcourt, Brace & World, 1959.

Schrecker, Ellen. *Many Are the Crimes: McCarthyism in America.* Boston: Little, Brown, 1998.

Smith, John Cabot. *Alger Hiss: The True Story.* New York: Penguin, 1977.

Tanenhaus, Sam. *Whittaker Chambers: A Biography.* New York: Random House, 1997.

Walker, Martin. *The Cold War: A History.* New York: Henry Holt, 1995.

Weinstein, Allen. *Perjury: The Hiss-Chambers Case.* New York: Random House, 1997.

THE TRIALS OF ZACARIAS MOUSSAOUI

Moussoaui, Abd Samad. *Zacarias, My Brother.* New York: Seven Stories Press, 2003.

The 9/11 Commission Report: Final Report of the National Commission on Terrorist Attacks upon the United States. Washington, DC: Government Printing Office, 2004. Available at www.gpoaccess.gov/911/pdf/fullreport.pdf.

Photo Credits

Index

Page numbers in italic typeface denote photographs or illustrations.